Living with Someone Who's Living with Bipolar Disorder

Living with Someone Who's Living with Bipolar Disorder

A Practical Guide for Family, Friends, and Coworkers

Chelsea Lowe and
Bruce M. Cohen, MD, PhD

JOSSEY-BASS
A Wiley Imprint
www.josseybass.com

Published by Jossey-Bass
A Wiley Imprint
989 Market Street, San Francisco, CA 94103-1741—www.josseybass.com

Jossey-Bass books and products are available through most bookstores. To contact Jossey-Bass directly call our Customer Care Department within the U.S. at 800-956-7739, outside the U.S. at 317-572-3986, or fax 317-572-4002.

Jossey-Bass also publishes its books in a variety of electronic formats. Some content that appears in print may not be available in electronic books.

Library of Congress Cataloging-in-Publication Data

Lowe, Chelsea.
  Living with someone who's living with bipolar disorder : a practical guide for family, friends, and coworkers / Chelsea Lowe and Bruce M. Cohen.
      p. cm.
  Includes bibliographical references and index.
  ISBN 978-0-470-47566-9 (pbk.)
1. Manic-depressive illness—Popular works.   I. Cohen, Bruce M.   II. Title.
  RC516.L69 2010
  616.89'5–dc22

                                                                              2009033973

Printed in the United States of America
FIRST EDITION
PB Printing 10 9 8 7 6 5 4 3 2 1

CONTENTS

*To our agent, Gina Panettieri—you rock!—and
to my six parental units
—Chelsea Lowe*

*To my mom and dad, who both in their own ways
spent their lives caring for others
—Bruce M. Cohen*

PREFACE

My very first psychiatric patient had a form of bipolar disorder. She was a brilliant young woman whose illness had disrupted her life, her career, and her relationships. Fortunately, her symptoms first waned and then vanished in the face of comprehensive treatment. Her astonishing experiences—of mood swings and delusions followed by sanity, of wild behaviors and speech that resolved to reveal a wise and thoughtful wife and mother—convinced me that I wanted to spend my career trying to understand and improve care for people with this fascinating condition.

For more than thirty years, I have specialized in the psychiatric treatment of patients with bipolar disorder. I have helped care for thousands of patients, and run a major hospital dedicated to those with psychiatric disorders. As a researcher, I have sought and still actively seek to develop new and better treatments. I have written many articles and chapters, both on my own work and to guide others studying and treating bipolar disorder. Along with many others in my field, I have kept looking for better ways to help.

Early in my career, I recognized the importance of including partners and relatives of the patient in my own care of those with psychiatric illnesses. Often my patients brought their partners to appointments; sometimes they were brought by their partners. I soon learned that things almost always went better when a partner was involved: I got more information; my patient got more help and support. After all, patients don't just need doctors. Yes, they need a thorough personal evaluation, followed by professional monitoring and treatment; but they also need a well-organized life. All these needs are best addressed with the involvement of people who care enough to learn about the illness and be part of the overall plan of treatment.

When Chelsea Lowe asked me to contribute to this book—written to address the needs of the partners of people living with bipolar disease—I thought she had a wonderful idea, and I was glad to help. As I spoke to patients and their partners, relatives, and friends, I had come to see the effects of bipolar disorder on them all. I realized that partners wanted to be involved and supportive, but didn't know how. They needed to know what was happening, what would make things better, what was dangerous and might make things worse, what roles they could play. Because they were affected, they needed to know; because they cared, they wanted to help.

Most people, however, know little about psychiatric disorders, and much of what is portrayed in movies or books serves a dramatic point and may not be accurate. There are many factual books, good ones, from brief to encyclopedic, on bipolar disorder. Some of these are listed in the Resources section at the end of this book. Mostly, these books were written by doctors or patients and for doctors or patients. Few, if any, were written for the partner of someone with bipolar disorder. Although much of what we each need to know is the same, not everything is. Partners have different experiences, a different role, and different needs than doctors or patients.

This book is written specifically for partners of people who suffer from bipolar disorder. We know from our own experiences that accurate information and good advice on bipolar disorder can lead to better relationships and more productive lives. We hope the information in this book will provide you with a solid foundation of understanding and will give you and your loved one useful guidance and assist you in understanding your options and accessing the resources you need.

Bruce M. Cohen

INTRODUCTION

Bipolar disorder, or BD, is common—many millions of people around the world have it, and millions more are diagnosed with it each year. We know from surveys that a great many people suffering from bipolar disorder go undiagnosed. Most of us, whether we realize it or not, know someone who is living with bipolar disorder—a colleague, a roommate, a friend. And many people live with someone who is living with BD—a partner, a parent, a child. Being part of the life of a bipolar person can be difficult, confusing, and frustrating. If we don't understand the disorder and how it affects our loved one, our relationships can easily spin out of control.

The symptoms of bipolar disorders—plural, because BD has many forms—can range from the wild behavioral extremes of mania (outrageous confidence, spending or gambling away fortunes, embarking on ill-conceived affairs, quitting steady work to pursue an irrational dream) to the quieter but equally troubling consequences of severe depression (immobilizing fatigue, deep sadness, overwhelming self-doubt, and loss of pleasure).

Often, partners and family members are surprised to discover that the person they've known for so long is in fact bipolar, not just difficult or moody. Cavernous depressions, irrational irritability, insistent speech that denies would-be conversational partners the chance to participate, disorderly thinking, poor judgment, resistance to help, and other symptoms can be trying for those close to an individual with bipolar disorder. More often than not, they have a difficult time finding a reliable source for information and support.

Yet for those whose lives are affected by bipolar disorder, these are good times to live in. Never before have people with BD enjoyed better access to adequate diagnoses, medications, and support. Never has awareness of the condition been greater. And for most individuals diagnosed with one of the various types of bipolar disorder, there is at least one other—a spouse, parent, child, sibling, or friend—who cares, wants to help, and desires, for themselves and their loved ones, to enjoy a fulfilling life and good relationships.

To this end, information—about bipolar disorder, about how it affects our loved ones—is vital: the more we have, the less we avoid, patronize, or stigmatize the person with BD, and the better able we are to deal, singly and together, with the problems that are bound to arise. People living with people who are living with BD need information and understanding, help and support, every day. That's why we wrote this book.

Living with Someone Who's Living with Bipolar Disorder is organized into two parts. The chapters in Part One, Understanding Bipolar Disorder, address the nature of this illness, a bit of its history, and the medication and treatment options available to those living with BD. The chapters in Part Two, Living with Your Partner, speak to the needs of the relationship and two people in it, particularly the partner—named in the title of this book—who is living with someone living with bipolar disorder.

ACKNOWLEDGMENTS

Writing a book is hard. Writing one with an actively involved coauthor is doubly so. I was truly fortunate to have been matched with Dr. Bruce M. Cohen, who immediately put the lie to any clichés about doctors and ego. I'm grateful for his kindness, patience, dedication to the work, and refusal to allow his name to appear before mine in the credits.

Adriana Bobinchock made my job infinitely easier, as she so often has. Gina Panettieri can't really be thanked enough. The same is true of Sallie Randolph, who showed extraordinary goodness in coming to my assistance.

Peter Pearson, PhD, director of the Couples Institute in Menlo Park, California, and Brian Quinn, LCSW, PhD, astonished me with their generosity of time and expertise. Drs. Jacqueline Olds, MD, and Tina B. Tessina, PhD, were similarly gracious, as were Dost Onger, MD, PhD, and Dr. Stephen J. Seiner, MD. Thanks also to the Social Security Administration, the office of the Equal Employment Opportunity Commission, NASA's Johnson Space Center, and the Federal Aviation Administration for putting up with my ignorance kindly and patiently. The City of Boston Women's Commission, the Massachusetts Department of Public Health, the Samaritans, the Depression and Bipolar Support Alliance, and the Academy of Cognitive Therapy were generous and kind as well.

Thanks also to the U.S. Substance Abuse Mental-Health System Administration and to Skenderian Apothecary, Cambridge, Massachusetts; Boston College; Karen Sontag; W. Thomas Smith Jr.; and Dr. Judith Beck.

Russell Wild, MBA, and Joel Schonfeld, JD, helped me understand the wherefores of lenders.

My gratitude goes, as always, to the American Society of Journalists and Authors, my sine qua non, and to Catherine

Wald, Patti McCracken, Erica Manfred, Nancy Peske, Stephanie Golden, and Alexandra Owens.

Thanks as well to Sergeant Jim Bailey, Drs. Jon and Jill Ladd, and Dr. Carolyn Maltas. And to my husband, as always, for his insight, support, advice, and killer sense of humor.

Thanks, most of all, to the men and women who shared their stories.

—Chelsea Lowe

I gratefully acknowledge:

Chelsea Lowe, for the idea and drive to write this book, for laying out all its initial content, for many hours of redrafting, and for asking me to join her in this work; Naomi Lucks, for reading the drafts comprehensively, asking good questions, making sure that all that needed to be said was said, and for expert and exceptional help in organizing and editing; Alan Rinzler, for appreciating the value of this project and shepherding it through to conclusion; my clinical colleagues Philip Levendusky, PhD, Dost Ongur, MD, PhD, Paul Barreira, MD, and Jean Frazier, MD, for input on technical aspects of bipolar disorder, its treatment, and resources to help patients and families; my colleagues at the Frazier Institute, Sue Babb, MS, and Cathie Bowen, for help with searches for information and with text preparation; Adriana Bobinchock, the head of McLean Public Relations, for help with contacts and for reading our drafts and advising on content; and my wife, Marian Cohen, PhD, professor of sociology, Framingham State College, for many insightful discussions on dealing with psychiatric disorders and other sources of stress and misbehavior in life.

—Bruce M. Cohen

Living with Someone Who's Living with Bipolar Disorder

Part 1

Understanding Bipolar Disorder

 **CHAPTER 1**

What Is (and Isn't) Bipolar Disorder?

Manic-depression distorts moods and thoughts, incites dreadful behaviors, destroys the basis of rational thought, and too often erodes the desire and will to live. It is an illness that is biological in its origins, yet one that feels psychological in the experience of it; an illness that is unique in conferring advantage and pleasure, yet one that brings in its wake almost unendurable suffering and, not infrequently, suicide.

I am fortunate that I have not died from my illness, fortunate in having received the best medical care available, and fortunate in having the friends, colleagues, and family that I do.
—Kay Redfield Jamison, PhD

Kay Redfield Jamison, who writes eloquently about her experience with bipolar disorder, credits others with helping sustain her. She knows very well that bipolar disorder doesn't affect only one person and is best managed by two or more people working together. Let's listen to the voices of people who are living with people with bipolar disorder:

My husband, Ryan, is manic-depressive, although I didn't know that when we got married. I thought he was just moody, and—I can't believe this—I thought it was kind of attractive; he was unpredictable and mysterious, like a romantic poet. But the poetry became work. And that's not even his depression phase—that's his manic mood! A lot of people think the manic side is happy. But his shrink told me that mania doesn't always look "happy, happy, happy." More often than not, it's irritability that explodes into rage. Great, right?
—*Jane Pastalouchi, Des Moines*

When my ex-girlfriend told me she was manic, I said, "No, you're totally out of control." And she was! In the summer especially, she could never sleep. So she'd spend hours roll-erblading—in the dark! Then *I* couldn't sleep because I was worried she'd fall and break something, or be attacked by someone less innocently out at night.
—*Harold Goldstein, New York City*

Jeff was hilarious—a really great guy to be around. He was so funny and so handsome—when we got dressed for a party, he was almost shiny, like a celebrity. He was kind of famous, actually—a pretty well-known photographer, and his output was phenomenal. But then, over the course of a week or so, he'd spiral down. The bottom would just drop out. He'd get so low he was unrecognizable, almost. He stopped working, shaving, bathing, even talking . . . he wouldn't change his clothes. He looked like a homeless person. Our kids thought it was like having two dads, and pretended it was funny, but it wasn't. Now, when my teenage grandson goes radio silent and shuts himself in his room, I wonder if it's happening all over again . . .
—*Helen Watchover, Los Angeles*

My wife seemed fine. She was great with our kids—lunches, school, homework. And I really depended on her to do that. Didn't think twice about it. When she was stressed, she'd cry a lot, but then she'd snap out of it, and she seemed really happy again—baking cookies, cleaning the house from top to bottom, cutting out a million coupons—the whole Mom thing. She went to therapy, sure, but who doesn't? Then one night before dinner she told me she wanted to die. She had it all planned out. I got really scared and called her therapist, he had her come in, and the next thing I knew she was hospitalized. Now she's on some kind of medication, and she seems pretty even, but sometimes I get scared that she'll stop taking it and want to kill herself again.
—Michael Jetter, St. Louis

Does any of this sound familiar?

If your partner or loved one is bipolar, you have your own stories to tell. You may be lucky enough to have found someone who'll listen, or you may feel too embarrassed and just hope the problem will go away. This suppression can make you feel isolated and alone. But although you may often feel isolated, you—and your partner—are far from alone.

Bipolar disorder—or more accurately *disorders*, as there are multiple types—is an often misunderstood and misdiagnosed group of illnesses believed, conservatively, to affect more than five million American adults. The National Alliance on Mental Illness, considering all of the bipolar and related disorders, puts the figure closer to ten million.

To give you some perspective on this number, approximately 2.2 million people over eighteen in the United States are thought to suffer from obsessive-compulsive disorder; 2.4 million from schizophrenia, 4.5 million from Alzheimer's disease; and about 18 million from diabetes. So yes, by any standard, there are a lot of people living with bipolar illness, and many more who are living with these folks.

What *is* bipolar disorder? Well, first, its name comes from its most obvious characteristic: people with bipolar disorder tend to experience extreme, polar opposite states of mood. They can be exceptionally high, or "manic," at one time, then exceptionally low, or "depressed," at other times. Although there is much more to BD, as you will see, the extreme moods are what people note most often.

As to cause, bipolar disorder is not your partner's "fault": it is a brain condition. It does not happen because of upbringing, although it can be triggered or worsened by physical or emotional trauma or extreme stress. (The same is true of many medical conditions, such as high blood pressure.) It does not happen because your partner wants it to, either.

Although it may not be chronic (meaning symptoms never go away), it is usually *recurrent* (that is, symptoms keep returning), and some symptoms can linger, even when someone with bipolar is not having a full episode of illness. To varying degrees, these symptoms and episodes can be managed. The most common treatments are medication, neurotherapies (physical treatments, other than drugs, to change brain activity), and supportive therapies (such as psychotherapy). We'll discuss all of these in greater detail later in this book.

In this chapter, however, we'll address the basic question: What does bipolar disorder look and feel like?

BIPOLAR DISORDERS

Bipolar disorder is characterized by its episodes of extremes in mood, and that's what people with BD actually experience. Understanding the nature of these moods makes it easier to understand the differences between the types of bipolar disorders.

Bipolar Moods

A *manic episode* is typified by elevated mood, increased energy, and perhaps paradoxically, irritability. Often there is a sense of power or importance, rapid thinking, talkativeness, a flurry of activity, and decreased need for sleep. There may be impaired thinking and psychotic symptoms (delusions and hallucinations). In a manic episode, symptoms are severe enough to cause substantial disruption to daily life and obligations. Sometimes hospitalization is required.

A *hypomanic* episode has the same basic features as a manic episode, only milder. By definition, hypomanic symptoms do not cause severe disability or hospitalization and are not associated with psychosis.

A *depressive* episode is characterized by sadness or low mood; diminished energy, interest, and pleasure; greater or lesser appetite for food; excessive or poor-quality sleep; and feelings of worthlessness or guilt, and even despair.

Mood swing means that the episodes of mania and depression shift from one pole to the other. This can happen over and over again. If the shifts occur at least four times a year, the illness is called *rapid cycling*.

A *mixed* episode is when mania and depression fluctuate so quickly that they seem to occur at the same time, or when symptoms that meet the criteria for a manic and a depressive episode actually do occur at the same time. Indeed, the "poles" of bipolar disorder are not entirely opposites; if you read about the symptoms, you will see they overlap.

Sometimes the term *mixed mania* is used when manic features predominate but there are also substantial symptoms of depression. Similarly, there are states of *energetic or agitated* depression—in which depression dominates but features of mania exist at the same time.

The Disorders

The most commonly used official diagnostic criteria for bipolar disorders are given in the American Psychiatric Association's *Diagnostic and Statistical Manual of Mental Disorders*, fourth edition, called by its initials: *DSM-IV-TR*—the principal guidebook for psychiatrists. (You'll find excerpts from the complete clinical criteria at the end of this book.) Although at first glance these criteria may seem clear, in practice a diagnosis of BD is not a simple one to make, primarily because BD is often confused with other disorders with similar features. In fact, it has been estimated that the average bipolar patient suffers through *ten years* of symptoms before receiving a correct diagnosis.

The *DSM-IV-TR* and most other official criteria recognize multiple forms of bipolar disorder. The primary forms are bipolar 1 and bipolar 2.

Bipolar 1 Disorder
According to the *DSM-IV-TR*,

> The essential feature of Bipolar I Disorder is a clinical course that is characterized by the occurrence of at least one, and usually more, so-called Manic Episodes or Mixed Episodes. Often individuals have already had one or more Major Depressive Episodes. Sometimes, the individual is experiencing a first episode of illness (i.e., Single Manic Episode). More commonly, the disorder is recurrent. Recurrence is indicated by either a shift in the polarity of the episode, from manic to depressed or vice versa, or by an interval between episodes of at least two months without symptoms of illness.

The illness is said to be chronic if an episode never fully ends, and significant symptoms remain; it is recurrent if there are new episodes of illness separated from previous episodes by at least a few months.

Bipolar 1 patients do not just have extremes of mood. They may also experience hallucinations and, more commonly, delusions. For this reason, BD is considered a psychosis.

Hallucinations are false sensory perceptions. In BD, these are usually auditory (such as hearing voices) or visual (seeing things that are not there). Often these voices or visions are related to the episode of illness. They are often consistent with the high mood and grandiosity of mania (the victim might believe she hears voices of angels or God), or with despondency in depression (the voices might tell him he is worthless or disgusting).

Delusions are false and odd beliefs. As with hallucinations, in BD they are often consistent with the prevailing mood. A person who is manic may believe he has exceptional, even superhuman, strength or prowess. An individual who is depressed might believe she is rotting or beset by demons. Delusions of grandeur or persecution are the most common delusions in people with bipolar 1 disorder. (We'll look at these in a little more detail later in this chapter.)

In lay terms, bipolar 1 is the classic form. It is what most people think of when they hear the terms *bipolar* or *manic-depressive*: the recurring experience of big highs (mania) and big lows (depression). But it is not the only type of bipolar disorder.

Bipolar 2 Disorder
According to the *DSM-IV-TR*, "The essential feature of Bipolar II Disorder is a clinical course that is characterized by the occurrence of one or more Major Depressive Episodes accompanied by at least one Hypomanic Episode."

Hypomania can be characterized by abundant energy, confidence, and other seemingly "good" emotions and states—or, like mania, it can be associated with disconcerting irritability. In people suffering from bipolar 2, this mood state often precedes an episode of serious depression.

A person suffering from bipolar 2 disorder may not appear to be as "clearly manic-depressive" to the observer, especially when the person just seems to be in a particularly good mood. But it can be just as serious a disorder as bipolar 1, because the depressions can be just as deep.

Is There a "Bipolar 3"?

Some people seem to experience episodes of bipolar disorder only in the context of a general medical illness, such as multiple sclerosis or thyroid disease, or only after exposure to a drug, such as a steroid medication or a stimulant. The term *bipolar 3* is often used to describe bipolar disorder apparently induced by prescription or nonprescription drugs.

Of particular importance, medication prescribed for a diagnosed depression will sometimes give rise to mania or hypomania instead of just restoring normal mood. This may be the first evidence that someone suffering a depression has a form of illness related to bipolar disorder. The relationship between these forms of the disorder and bipolar 1 and 2 is not clear; but, in addition to symptoms, all probably share some underlying physical characteristics, including inherited factors that determine the risks of becoming ill.

Human conditions are rarely fully described by neat lists of symptoms and specific criteria, and so it is with bipolar disorder. Many people have symptoms of BD, but don't quite fit the criteria in the textbooks. The *DSM-IV-TR* classifies such people as *Bipolar Disorder Not Otherwise Specified, or BD-NOS*, another term you may have heard. People who have BD-NOS can experience some or most of the elements of mania and depression, but not enough to meet the specific criteria for Bipolar 1 or 2 Disorder in the *DSM-IV-TR. Cyclothymia* is frequently found in relatives of people who have bipolar disorder. This much milder version of BD includes both depressions and hypomanias, and mood may shift much more rapidly than in other forms of bipolar disorder. Although less severe than bipolar 1 and 2, it can cause problems in daily life and relationships. Over time, it may evolve into other forms of BD.

So: Is there really a bipolar 3? There is no consensus on this issue. Some people speak of bipolar 3 and even 4 and 5, but there is no general agreement as to use. The *DSM-IV-TR* does not use "bipolar 3." These terms can mean different things to different experts.

GOING TO EXTREMES: BIPOLAR BEHAVIORS

Most of us have restless nights when we can't sleep, days when we feel irritable and touchy, moments of being impulsive or doing something that in retrospect seems foolish. For people with bipolar disorder, however, these common occurrences become magnified.

People who have bipolar disorder are more likely, when manic, to engage in all kinds of dangerous activities—from embarking on affairs to engaging prostitutes to driving recklessly or running around dodgy neighborhoods in the middle of the night to quitting needed jobs with no thought about the consequences. People with untreated BD may even commit crimes or impulsively injure themselves or others, as a consequence of their illness. (In fact, an estimated forty thousand people in the U.S. prison system suffer from bipolar disorder.)

You might notice that your spouse or partner constantly seems to invade your privacy—opening your mail or e-mail, listening in on private conversations, or asking invasive questions. Intense curiosity can also be a part of bipolar disorder.

For some people who have bipolar disorder, self-centeredness can be extreme. A bipolar person might not see his or her viewpoint as the right one, so much as the *only* one. You might sometimes find, to your frustration, that your feelings, opinions, wishes, and conversation hardly seem to matter. When ill, your partner might appear blatantly selfish. Your partner might also misunderstand things you or others do or say, or give such convoluted rationales for his own actions or thoughts as to leave you shaking your head—or banging it (figuratively, we hope) into the nearest wall.

Even more frustrating for their partners, people who have bipolar disorder often don't believe that their extreme moods and unusual behaviors are part of an illness—or even abnormal. A bipolar person may not feel distressed or may believe that his distress is only circumstantial, that a new job or the improvement of a stressful situation (or you!) would make the problems disappear. Doctors call this a "lack of insight."

To someone with bipolar disorder, BD is mostly about extreme moods and altered thinking. To the rest of us, it's about the behaviors that go with those symptoms. Understanding the types of behaviors that are typical of bipolar illness might help you understand and talk to your spouse or partner about his symptoms, actions, and beliefs. Let's look at a few of the more common and obvious behaviors.

Sleeplessness

During manic episodes, along with increased energy and activity throughout the day, wakefulness is common. Bipolar sufferers may report not feeling the need to sleep or being kept awake by tormented, "racing"—that is, rapid, numerous, and changing—thoughts. They might even stay awake, or mostly so, for days at a time—which can lead to dangerous physical exhaustion and contribute to many other extreme behaviors. Or they may sleep for only an hour or two a night—then make up the loss by sleeping away the better part of a day or two.

Extreme Irritability

If you're living with someone who's living with bipolar disorder, you've no doubt noticed extreme irritability—or downright nastiness—creeping into your conversations, perhaps for prolonged periods. Often these statements and behaviors are exaggerated reactions to real events or annoyances; sometimes they're irrational, and would look that way to any observer. During these times, you or others might be subjected to seemingly nonsensical rants, blame throwing, and verbal threats or challenges. You may even be subject to inappropriate physical actions, such as breaking or throwing objects, or even assault.

You might also notice undue anger. We're not talking about the angry feelings most people experience from day to day, but extreme displeasure, criticism, or irrational fury directed at life in general, a frustrating situation, or you in particular. You might be accused of having done something "wrong." You might also get blamed for far more than you deserve. You may feel as if—at least, in the eyes of your spouse—you can do nothing right.

 LIVING WITH BD

Bob and Tanya

For ten years of marriage I've adjusted my behavior to my wife's outbursts. I figured that I must be the cause of her rage—I know I can be sloppy, I don't always pick up after myself, sometimes I

(continued)

(*continued*)

forget to lock the door when I go out . . . you know, stuff like that. Tanya constantly picks fights with me about my short-comings—of course, she calls them something worse than that—and I always apologize and promise to do better, but there's always something.

That's bad enough. But the really annoying thing is that after she's gotten it all off her chest, and I'm just exhausted from the whole thing, she's all sunny smiles and energy. If I criticize her, I get another earful as to how wrong I am.

Extreme Talkativeness

Many people who suffer from BD talk incessantly during manic phases. People who have bipolar 1 may even talk themselves hoarse! (That doesn't necessarily end the behavior, however.) To a lesser degree, they may become abnormally "chatty," oblivious to the fact that another person who may wish to join in the conversation can't get a word in.

Distractibility, Tangentiality, and Inability to Concentrate

A person with BD can switch hastily and frequently from one project to another. Psychiatrists call this *distractibility*, an apt description. Your partner may begin to fix a leaky pipe, for example, only to drop all the tools on the floor and begin working at the computer on a writing project, only to become engrossed a short while later in cleaning the mildew from the shower.

You might also notice the person changing topics rapidly or drifting quickly away from the subject at hand. (Psychiatrists call this *tangentiality*.) The speaker might seem to jump from point to point without necessarily taking the listener along, which can be disorienting if you are seriously trying to follow the train of thought.

Overspending and Excessive Gambling

Overspending is a problem frequently seen in people who have bipolar disorder, and one that can wreak havoc in a relationship based on shared finances. Some of the stories seem too fantastic to be true: a man buys two new Maseratis in one day (and doesn't even have a driver's license!). A woman flies to Las Vegas at the spur of the moment and proceeds to lose $15,000 in an afternoon. A grandmother of six stays in the house all day wearing the same sweat suit while purchasing thousands of dollars worth of clothing (delivered, but unopened and never returned) from a home shopping channel on television. A man goes to the grocery store and spends hundreds of dollars on exotic fruits and vegetables that go bad quickly because his refrigerator is already stuffed full of uneaten groceries.

Hypersexuality

Some people who are bipolar find themselves overwhelmed with sexual thoughts and impulses during manic episodes. This can lead to unhealthy affairs, marital tensions, and breakups. One man reports that during manic episodes, his wife not only demanded sex from him several times a day but regularly had four or five casual affairs with men she barely knew. (Conversely, a very depressed partner might, for long stretches, demonstrate virtually no interest in sex.)

Substance Abuse

Substance abuse can be a sign of bipolar disorder. It is important to be aware that people with BD often use sedatives for sleep, alcohol for anxiety, and stimulants to raise mood. In part, they are probably treating their symptoms; in part, they are exercising the bad judgment and impulsivity typical of BD.

What Are the Symptoms of Bipolar Disorder?

According to the National Institute of Mental Health, these changes in behavior and mood may signal bipolar disorder.

Signs and symptoms of mania (or a *manic episode*) include the following:

- Increased energy, activity, and restlessness
- Excessively "high," overly good, euphoric mood
- Extreme irritability
- Racing thoughts and talking very fast, jumping from one idea to another
- Distractibility; can't concentrate well
- Little sleep needed
- Unrealistic beliefs in one's abilities and powers
- Poor judgment
- Spending sprees
- A lasting period of behavior that is different from usual
- Increased sexual drive
- Abuse of drugs, particularly cocaine, alcohol, and sleeping medications
- Provocative, intrusive, or aggressive behavior
- Denial that anything is wrong
- A manic episode is diagnosed if elevated mood occurs with three or more of the other symptoms most of the day, nearly every day, for one week or longer. If the mood is irritable, four additional symptoms must be present.

Signs and symptoms of depression (or a *depressive episode*) include the following:

- Lasting sad, anxious, or empty mood
- Feelings of hopelessness or pessimism
- Feelings of guilt, worthlessness, or helplessness

- Loss of interest or pleasure in activities once enjoyed, including sex
- Decreased energy; a feeling of fatigue or of being "slowed down"
- Difficulty concentrating, remembering, making decisions
- Restlessness or irritability
- Sleeping too much, or can't sleep
- Change in appetite and/or unintended weight loss or gain
- Chronic pain or other persistent bodily symptoms that are not caused by physical illness or injury
- Thoughts of death or suicide, or suicide attempts

PSYCHOTIC SYMPTOMS

Psychotic symptoms—the most common being delusions of grandeur or persecution—can be very upsetting. During a manic episode, people often believe themselves capable of much more than they are. They might suddenly think they possess great brilliance, insight, or other intellectual abilities or great strength or physical skills. Such enthusiasm and unquestioning belief in the truth of what they are saying can be hard to resist, especially the first time you experience it. It can also be dangerous.

Perhaps your partner managed to convince you, during such an episode, that your money problems were—or soon would be—over, or that a great opportunity beckoned, just over the horizon. You might get swept up into investing time, enthusiasm, or money, only to find yourself disappointed later, when the "opportunity" fails to materialize.

Delusions can cause the sufferer to make irrational decisions. She might suddenly drop a long-term friendship, saying her former friend has been systematically poisoning her friends against her. Or he might quit his job because he *knows* he will be offered the chance of a lifetime later this afternoon. One woman told her boyfriend that she had to break off their relationship that afternoon because it was critical for her to move to Mexico *that day* to open a spiritually based health care clinic that would save humankind from the coming plague.

Your partner's delusions could be considerably more disturbing. She might tell you that others are "persecuting" or keeping watch over her or even controlling her, sending her secret messages in the daily newspaper, with which she has papered the walls of the bathroom. One man described having the conviction that he was Truman in *The Truman Show*—watched by TV cameras and living a scripted life, and that he might have to kill the director.

If you have ever witnessed your spouse or partner in the grip of a paranoid delusion—suddenly swearing that he's being watched or monitored, or making unfounded accusations toward you or others—you know how frightening such an episode can be.

In the late nineteenth century, a German psychiatrist named Dr. Emil Kraepelin (1856–1926), after observing thousands of patients with the same troubling symptoms, coined the term *manic-depressive illness*. He also made many of the distinctions that became the basis of what we now call bipolar disorder (somewhat similar to what he called "manic depression") and schizophrenia (somewhat similar to what he called "dementia praecox"). This marked a milestone in our modern understanding of bipolar disorder. But human awareness of the condition, as we will see in the next chapter, goes back much farther.

CHAPTER 2

A Brief, Colorful History (and Some Science) of Bipolar Disorder

Had [Winston Churchill] been a stable and equable man, he could never have inspired the nation. In 1940, when all the odds were against Britain, a leader of sober judgment might well have concluded that we were finished.
—Anthony Storr (1920–2001)

Even a cursory glance at the history of bipolar disorder tells us one very important fact: bipolar individuals are and have always been a part of our society. Despite the demonization and stigmatization of the mentally ill throughout human history, most have played typical roles, and their illness was little noted. It is also clear that some people struggling with bipolar disorder or those believed to have been bipolar—from Beethoven to Winston Churchill, Dick Cavett, and Francis Ford Coppola—have played vital roles in human history and made enormous contributions to culture. Of course, they were usually most productive when their symptoms were absent or minimal. It has only been recently—since the second half of the twentieth century, in fact—that doctors could begin to effectively *treat* the most serious symptoms of BD. Management of the illness today is still not perfect, but it is a long way ahead of where it once was.

FROM MANIA AND MELANCHOLIA TO BIPOLAR DISORDER

Physicians as far back as ancient Greece recognized BD's two emotional and behavioral extremes as one illness—and recorded its symptoms with uncanny accuracy. In particular, Aretaeus of Cappadocia (a part of modern Turkey), believed to have lived in the first century (c. 30–90), described patients who "desired to die" or became "dispirited" and "sleepless." His description could be used today: "Melancholia is the beginning and a part of mania. . . . The development of a mania is really a worsening of the disease (melancholia) rather than a change into another disease." He also noted the increased sexuality of mania, among other symptoms we still recognize today, and made the connection between *mania* (the term he used) and *melancholia* (his term for depression).

Aretaeus had been influenced by the so-called father of medicine, Hippocrates (c. BCE 460 – c. BCE 370), who saw illnesses as physical, caused by bodily imbalances, rather than rooted in the spirit world. Hippocrates taught that disorders of mood and thinking were illnesses of the brain. Other descriptions of what we might now call bipolar disorder appear in ancient Egyptian papyri, in the religious and medical texts of ancient India, and in the Old and New Testaments of the Bible, from King David and Job to many (if not all) of the prophets. For example, Elijah wins a victory over 450 prophets of Baal—outrunning chariots in the process!—and then expresses the desire to give up and die (1 Kings 19).

The Middle Ages

During the Middle Ages in Europe, the mentally ill were often not as fortunate as they had been during the time of Aretaeus and other physicians who believed in physical causes for mental disorders. Some groups showed understanding and compassion, but others as late as the 1600s believed that the mentally ill were suffering from demonic possession or witches' spells.

Some monasteries and towns offered asylum to those with mental illnesses, including bipolar disorder; and many Muslim groups in the Middle East believed in compassionate care, establishing asylums as early as the 900s. But throughout most of this period, care for mentally disturbed persons generally fell to families. Some patients received kind treatment, but many were imprisoned or brutally mistreated. So little was understood about mental illness, or known about how to treat it, that psychotic individuals often were chained down in their homes. (It is from this and similar later practices that the expression "fit to be tied" derives.) Europeans in urban areas sometimes depended on workhouses or alms houses for such patients. Then, as now, many of the mentally ill joined the homeless. Then, as now, many found themselves in jail.

Renaissance and Enlightenment

The Renaissance was not necessarily a time of rebirth in compassionate care for people with mental disorders. Delusions, hallucinations, and other behavioral abnormalities often remained associated with witches, demonic possession, or devil worship—and punished accordingly. However, beginning in the 1600s, many European physicians once again began to advocate a physical-illness model and humane treatment.

The 1700s saw the rise of institutional asylums in Europe—but such places, including Bethlem in London, had existed in smaller form since medieval times. (In fact, Bethlem—the full name of which is the Priory of St. Mary at Bethlehem—was established in the early 1400s. It is from this facility that the term *bedlam*, to describe chaos and madness, originates.)

Later in the century in France, Dr. Philippe Pinel instituted reforms during his tenure at the Bicêtre asylum in Paris. Patients no longer were chained in dungeons but allowed sunny rooms and exercise. That period saw a number of reforms elsewhere in Europe as well.

The Nineteenth Century

In the United States, asylums were established on the European model, and care was based on the moral (humane) treatment advocated by Pinel. Reformer and physician Benjamin Rush instituted noteworthy advances at the Pennsylvania Hospital, although such practices as the use of restraints and bleeding remained. In the early 1800s, the Quakers (known as "Friends") established one of the first American private mental hospitals in Philadelphia. In 1811, when Massachusetts established its first public hospital, the Massachusetts General Hospital, the first division opened was a psychiatric asylum that became McLean Hospital.

In 1841, American educator and reformer Dorothea Dix chronicled the disgraceful conditions she saw psychiatric patients endure in a Massachusetts prison. Dix was so shaken that she spent the rest of her life fighting to improve the treatment of the mentally ill.

Forty-six years later, groundbreaking journalist Nellie Bly (nee Elizabeth Jane Cochran) would feign insanity to report undercover from inside the Women's Lunatic Asylum on Blackwell's Island in New York. In plain but eloquent language, she described conditions that call to mind the brutality of prison camps. The contributions of Dix and Bly helped bring inhuman conditions to light and facilitate reform.

Nellie Bly Reports on Life in the "Madhouse"

I could not sleep, so I lay in bed picturing to myself the horrors in case a fire should break out in the asylum. Every door is locked separately and the windows are heavily barred, so that escape is impossible. In the one building alone there are, I think Dr. Ingram told me, some three hundred women. They are locked, one to ten to a room. It is impossible to get out unless these doors are unlocked. A fire is not improbable, but one of the most likely occurrences. Should the building burn, the jailers or nurses would never think of releasing their crazy patients. This I can prove to you later when I come to tell of their cruel treatment of the poor things intrusted to their care. As I say, in case of fire, not a dozen women could escape. All would be left to roast to death. Even if the nurses were kind, which they are not, it would require more presence of mind than women of their class possess to risk the flames and their own lives while they unlocked the hundred doors for the insane prisoners. Unless there is a change there will some day be a tale of horror never equaled.

In this connection is an amusing incident which happened just previous to my release. I was talking with Dr. Ingram about many things, and at last told him what I thought would be the result of a fire.

"The nurses are expected to open the doors," he said.

"But you know positively that they would not wait to do that," I said, "and these women would burn to death."

He sat silent, unable to contradict my assertion.

(*continued*)

> (*continued*)
> "Why don't you have it changed?" I asked.
>   "What can I do?" he replied. "I offer suggestions until my brain is tired, but what good does it do? What would you do?" he asked, turning to me, the proclaimed insane girl.
> —NELLIE BLY, EXCERPT FROM *TEN DAYS IN A MADHOUSE*

The Twentieth Century

By the end of the nineteenth century and the beginning of the twentieth, patients in asylums, sanatoria, and similar institutions received somewhat more compassionate—but no more effective—treatment. At best, these establishments could do little more than care for their patients physically or offer comforting activities—not in themselves all that effective against bipolar disorder or other major mental illnesses.

By this time, psychiatrist Jean-Pierre Falret, who had named bipolar disorder *folie circulaire*, or "circular insanity" in his native French, in the 1850s, already understood the disorder had a genetic component, as did Dr. Kraepelin, late in the nineteenth and early in the twentieth century. Sigmund Freud, who began his career working on a physical model to explain mental disorders, had abandoned his early efforts and turned to working on the consequences of traumatic experiences and the structure of the human psyche.

Dr. Freud, the founder of the psychoanalytic school of psychology, proposed that "manic depression" grew, in part, out of early experiences and intrapsychic conflicts. (Thousands of years earlier, Plato had thought the same.) The "talking cure" model to reveal and treat psychological conflicts was attempted extensively for bipolar and other severe psychiatric disorders. (Until rather recently, psychologists and psychiatrists tried to treat these conditions primarily with psychotherapy, and elements of these approaches are still useful in treatment, as described later in this book.) By the end of his career, however, Freud returned to his earlier opinion that manic-depression and other psychotic illnesses were more likely brain disorders that would someday be treated with medications.

Not only doctors but also patients and their families began to be more public and active with regard to mental illness. In 1908, former mental patient Clifford Beers detailed his experiences in *A Mind That Found Itself*: "Soon," he wrote, "my disordered brain was busy with schemes for death. . . . My imaginary attacks were now occurring with distracting frequency, and I was in constant fear of discovery. During these three or four days I slept scarcely at all—even the medicine given to induce sleep having little effect." The following year, he established the National Committee for Mental Hygiene, an advocacy and prevention organization that, by the end of the twentieth century, had been followed by numerous others, described later in this book.

The 1930s saw the rise of sedative drugs, largely ineffectual for bipolar disorder; electroconvulsive therapy, effective for bipolar disorder, although initially dangerously primitive; and lobotomies, largely unsuccessful and often disabling, in attempts to control many kinds of mental illness symptoms.

In the 1940s, after World War II, the National Institutes of Health, including a mental health division, were established in the United States. Similar efforts to bring more science to medicine, including psychiatric medicine, were begun in many countries. These initiatives were based on the realization of how commonplace were various disorders, both psychiatric and purely physical, among soldiers. They were also based on a new appreciation of the power of science to advance technology, as demonstrated by weapons development during the war.

The Advent of Lithium

The ability of lithium to calm mania was not unknown, even to the ancients. Aretaeus recommended spring waters, which happened to contain lithium, for the treatment of mania. More recently, "lithiated water" enjoyed something of a health vogue in the 1800s. But it wasn't until the 1940s that science took it up in earnest.

While looking for a biologically based treatment for bipolar disorder, Australian doctor John F. J. Cade made the discovery of the element lithium as a calming agent. Within a short time, a small number of manic patients had responded dramatically to the drug. Dr. Cade reported having taken it himself first, to ensure that there were no harmful side effects (an approach now frowned upon and even illegal in many places).

However, it was not until the 1950s, when Danish researcher Dr. Mogens Schou followed up on Dr. Cade's studies, that lithium became better established. Schou's research was in part personally motivated. He had many family members who suffered from bipolar disorder.

In the 1970s, when lithium was first approved to treat mania and, later, to prevent bipolar symptoms, dosages were higher, forcing many patients into an unhappy choice: suffer from side effects or from the symptoms of the disorder itself. (Currently, dosages have been reduced, and blood levels and side effects are monitored to guide adjustments that keep doses from being too high.) For many, despite side effects, lithium was a lifesaver. Publisher Robert Giroux said of poet Robert Lowell, "Of all our conversations, I remember most vividly [Lowell's] words about the new drug, lithium carbonate, which had such good results and gave him reason to believe he was cured: 'It's terrible, Bob, to think that all I've suffered, and all the suffering I've caused, might have arisen from the lack of a little salt in my brain.'" (In fact, contrary to Lowell's under-standing, lithium for BD isn't a replacement therapy. Lithium levels in the body are miniscule under normal circumstances, and BD isn't a lithium deficiency disease. Lithium works as a drug, not a nutrient.)

Bipolar Disorder and the Media

By the end of the century, with improvements in understand-ing and treatment, bipolar disorder had hit mainstream culture and the media. Actor Richard Gere's character in the 1993 film *Mr. Jones* has been popularly interpreted as bipolar. NBC's long-running hospital drama *ER* featured two bipolar charac-ters. MTV, the BBC, and several major networks have aired specials on BD. It was only a matter of time before television saw its first bipolar detective in a prime-time police drama. Actor Gary Sweet joined the Australian TV show *Stingers* in its third season as bipolar detective Luke Harris. Sweet reported having visited a psychiatrist to prepare for the role—and concluded he was bipolar himself!

General Hospital soap star Maurice Bernard made his bipolar disorder public when it became part of his character, Sonny's, story line. Bernard has gone on to speak publicly about bipolar disorder and the importance of managing the illness. He also won a Prism award for his portrayal.

Former Columbia University student Lizzie Simon, now a writer, speaker, and consultant, wrote a book called *Detour: My Bipolar Road Trip in 4-D*, about her experiences and those of other young, successful people who have bipolar disorder. Simon has given numerous talks on the subject, and served as field producer for the MTV documentary *True Life: I'm Bipolar*.

It's fair to say that as awareness of bipolar disorder devel-ops, so too will sensitive and accurate portrayals in the media.

A Very Partial List of Famous People Who Are, Were, or May Have Been Bipolar

- **Politicians:** Sir Winston Churchill, Thomas Eagleton, Theodore Roosevelt, Abbie Hoffman
- **Artists and musicians:** Ludwig van Beethoven, Pyotr Illyich Tchaikovsky, Georg Friedrich Handel, Robert Schumann, Vincent van Gogh, Noel Coward, Cole Porter, Irving Berlin, Oscar Levant, Marilyn Monroe, Rosemary Clooney, Charlie Pride, Brian Wilson, Axl Rose, Francisco Scavullo, Frances Ford Coppola, Sinéad O'Connor, Susannah McCorkle, Kurt Cobain, Brittany Spears
- **Writers and journalists:** Honoré de Balzac, Edgar Allen Poe, Mark Twain, Charles Dickens, Emily Dickinson, Virginia Woolf, Graham Greene, Robert Lowell, Sylvia Plath, John Berryman, Jane Pauley
- **Theater:** Vivian Leigh, Moss Hart, Dick Cavett, Burgess Meredith, Patty Duke, Mariette Hartley, Margot Kidder, Carrie Fisher, Linda Hamilton

What We Believe Today

Advances in medical technologies, prominently including human genetics and brain imaging, are beginning to reveal evidence about the specific inherited and environmental factors determining risk for BD, as well as the physical differences in body and brain that mediate its symptoms. Many researchers believe that in the not-distant future, bipolar disorder will be diagnosed by blood tests and brain scans. It may also become possible one day to predict—and even prevent—its development.

Like high blood pressure or cardiovascular disease, bipolar disorder is determined both by what we inherit and by our life experiences. Its course is affected by how healthy we can keep the organ in which the illness occurs—the brain. Understanding the role of inheritance and what may be happening in the brains of people who have bipolar disorder can help in everything from evaluating the role of medication and supportive therapies in treating it to deciding when and whether to have children or take on any new challenge. For these reasons, we devote the rest of this chapter to basic information on the biology of bipolar disorder, and the consequences of this biology.

THE BIOLOGY OF BIPOLAR DISORDER

As in many medical conditions, heredity plays an important part in bipolar disorders. In fact, it is a stronger determinant of illness for BD than it is for most diseases and conditions. This observation, that bipolar disorders are caused by genes, is not controversial. It is proven. Many studies involving families, twins, and adoption have demonstrated that the risk of developing bipolar disorder is substantially determined by inherited factors.

Because bipolar disorders are inherited, they are frequently seen in related persons, especially close relatives, in whom the rate of similar illness may be higher than one in four. This increased prevalence of illness—not only bipolar disorder but also depression and other psychiatric disorders—is seen in relatives on both the mother's and father's sides of the families of people who have bipolar disorder.

One reason is that risk for BD is not determined predominantly by a single gene, inherited from one parent. Rather, in most cases, risk appears to be determined by the combined effect of numerous interacting genes, and relevant genetic material is inherited from both sides of the family. Thus it would be wrong to think that one parent deserves blame or guilt for transmitting the disorder. Assigning such blame is not only hurtful but also incorrect!

LIVING WITH BD

Andrea and Joe

We met in our late twenties, about twenty years ago. I didn't know anything about mood disorders. Joe was passionate and fascinating—a singer and songwriter—and I fell madly in love.

Neither of us had much awareness about mental health issues. I knew he was brilliant, creative, and artistic, I knew he would get really down sometimes, really sad. And I knew that he was an extremely mean drunk.

Later, when I got to know his family, I found out that his parents were both alcoholics. His sister, who lives in France, came for a visit, and told me that she had been diagnosed with bipolar disorder when she was a teenager, and had been on mood stabilizers for years. She clued me in that there was more going on with Joe than just moods, and we agreed that he needed more help than I could give him.

We finally talked Joe into seeing a psychiatrist, and he was treated for depression. He started out on Prozac. It helped for a while, but the mood swings came back and got much worse. Finally, he was diagnosed with BD, and we're still working on getting the medication right.

Like a lot of bipolar people, Joe self-medicated for years with alcohol, and still does occasionally. It's been a touchy issue with him. For a long time, he did not want to accept that his feelings were anything other than reactions to things that were happening in his life at the time. I get it, I really do—it's scary to know you're born with talents and limitations, and especially that you're not fully in control of things that are going on in your head.

Inherited Factors

Searches for the specific inherited factors involved have not yet led to definitive findings about exactly which genes are important in the cause of bipolar disorder, although several regions of the human genome appear to harbor genes that contribute to the risk. Notably, there is evidence that the particular genes in question include some that contain information related to brain cell growth. Others are for factors that control connections between brain cells. Several genes of interest determine the levels of elements, chemicals and their targets, that are used for communication of signals between and within brain cells.

Consistent with the results of the earlier family studies, newer gene finding analyses observe that the effect of each individual gene on overall risk seems small. For each one of us, it is the combined interactions of the multiple genes we inherit, some increasing risk and some decreasing it, that determine the overall likelihood that we will develop the disorder.

One controversial but important point concerns other roles the genes involved in determining BD may play in those who do *not* have the disorder. These same genes are likely to be involved in many normal brain functions. Also, because numerous genes are involved, they may (in some combinations) lead to greater or lesser emotionality or creativity, or other brain activities and mental states . . . but not to BD. Probably, most genes increase the risk for bipolar only when present in certain specific combinations.

And they do all of this indirectly: genes do not determine illness or health, but rather, the type and amount of proteins and other basic building blocks of the brain and other organs. They interact not only with one another but with all sorts of environmental factors. The physical features and functions of our brains are a complex outcome of all these elements acting together.

The Bipolar Brain: Physical Evidence

Progress in brain imaging supports the findings of gene research, providing clear evidence that bipolar disorders are a physically based disorder of the brain. As of now, no particular abnormality in the brain will definitively identify a person as having bipolar disorder. However, there are several specific features of the brain that are different, on average, in people who have the disorder as opposed to those who do not. Examples of these differences include the following results from studies of brain structure, chemistry, and function:

Four independent studies of the brain have reported a reduction of the cells called *glia* in the prefrontal cortex of the brain in people who have bipolar disorder. The prefrontal cortex, which sits at the very front of the brain, is involved in decision making and impulse control, and regulates activities related to setting mood and reward, among other functions.

Glia support the activity of nerve cells. Any reduction in glia could cause nerve cell dysfunction in the brain. This particular finding is from postmortem brains (that is, those studied after death), but scientists are working on ways to measure glial cells in the brain during subjects' lifetimes.

Studies using magnetic resonance imaging (MRI) have repeatedly observed abnormalities in patients with BD, including overactivity and possible enlargement in the brain region called the amygdala. The amygdala, located in the front end of the temporal lobe on the side of the brain, is one source of the "flight or fight" response—a long-standing and early part of our brain's evolution. More generally, it's involved in assessing danger and controlling fear and anxiety, functions that make its activities pertinent indeed to symptoms of BD.

The cerebellum, which sits at the back of the skull at the base of the brain, also seems abnormal in size and function in patients who have bipolar disorder. The cerebellum helps control the coordinated rhythms and patterns of activity of the brain, and disruptions of its functions may underlie various features of BD, from altered thinking to altered daily sleep and wakefulness patterns.

To perform its work, which involves both electrical and chemical activity, the brain uses ten times the energy, on average, of the rest of the body. There is growing evidence that one factor underlying BD is an inability to produce all the energy needed to run the brain. Most of this energy is produced in specialized organelles (meaning literally "tiny organs") called mitochondria inside our cells. Findings from brain imaging, genetic, and microscopic studies all agree that there are probably mitochondrial abnormalities in patients who have BD.

These are just some examples of physical differences in the brain seen in people with bipolar disorder. They may explain or contribute to the alterations in mood, thinking, and behavior that are key aspects of the disorder.

Participate in a Study

Academic centers all over the country and the world are performing studies of the causes of BD. Ultimately, the goal of these studies is to better understand BD and design better treatments for the disorder. People with BD can be part of this important work by volunteering for such studies. So can their family members. Specific opportunities can be found by contacting local academic medical centers or the National Institute of Mental Health (NIMH). Visit NIMH's clinical trials Web page (http://www.nimh.nih.gov/health/trials/index.shtml) or contact NIMH.

PROMISE FOR THE FUTURE

Unlike some inherited brain disorders—such as Huntington's disease, which is determined by a single gene—bipolar disorder is determined by many genes. Unlike many brain disorders—such as a tumor or stroke—BD is not localized to one part of the brain. It involves abnormalities of several regions or diffuse functions. This may make the condition harder for investigators to study, but it also suggests that there will be many routes to understanding it and many ways to help improve brain function to ameliorate or eliminate its symptoms in the future.

Teams of scientists are currently working in many centers on each of the findings and approaches we've noted in this chapter, and on many other leads and techniques we don't have space to mention. Progress is to be expected, which may produce very different and much more effective ways to diagnose and treat, or even prevent, the development of BD.

In the next chapter, we'll look at the diagnosis and treatment of bipolar disorders. By now, however, it should be abundantly clear that BD is not simple in its cause or its expression, so it will not surprise you that it is not an easy illness to diagnose or treat.

CHAPTER 3

Getting an Accurate Diagnosis

In 1994, I was going through a terrible divorce and someone said I needed to get help. . . . I ended up in the doctor's office, and he immediately assumed I was depressed. So I started on a round of anti-depressants but that caused me to go into a manic state. That was when I first really began realizing that something else was going on.
—Mariette Hartley, actress and national spokesperson for the American Foundation for Suicide Prevention

It's common for partners of people with BD to wonder, "Is my partner bipolar, or is this just his [or her] personality?"

Extremes of mood, especially mania, tend to exaggerate personality traits. Bipolar disorder can make people appear cranky, selfish, immature, self-indulgent, controlling, irrational, and morose. BD can make your partner go silent, be unkind or critical, or rage. It can lead those affected to abuse alcohol and drugs. All these behaviors can also be observed in people who are not bipolar, too. From time to time, we all behave poorly in some way.

So how can you know if your partner's behavior is caused by bipolar disorder or by other issues? On your own, you can't. That's why it's important to seek an accurate diagnosis from a qualified professional.

BIPOLAR DISORDER CAN BE DIFFICULT TO DIAGNOSE

One of the more frustrating situations encountered by partners of bipolar people—especially those with bipolar 2, the symptoms of which are not always as dramatic and clear-cut—is difficulty of diagnosis. Depression is the most common misdiagnosis—though that is changing, as bipolar disorder becomes better understood and publicized. Although bipolar depression and nonbipolar depression (so-called major depression in the United States, and unipolar depression most other places) share many symptoms and aspects of brain function, they are not exactly the same.

Another common misdiagnosis is attention deficit disorder (ADD) or attention deficit hyperactivity disorder (the same, with hyperactivity) (ADHD). This is because bipolar disorder shares some symptoms and probably even causal factors with ADD. In fact, areas of the brain that show altered function in bipolar disorder also control things like attention.

Further complicating diagnosis is the fact that BD is generally a "relapsing and remitting" disorder—its symptoms sometimes abate temporarily. When symptoms are not present, bipolar disorder can be missed.

These and other issues make bipolar disorder difficult to diagnose. One doctor may see evidence for bipolar 2, while another sees signs of agitated depression. Because bipolar often "presents" (professional jargon for the behaviors we see) as depression, other symptoms of BD may be overlooked. Fortunately, this doesn't happen as often as it once did.

LIVING WITH BD

Bill and Julia

Julia and I have been married just over forty years—and it wasn't until twenty-five years after we met that we got a diagnosis. When we were dating, Julia would go through brief, unexplained periods of depression that made me wonder whether something was seriously wrong. Later, those low periods lasted for weeks, but I figured they were just part of the package that was Julia—everyone's got their quirks.

Anyway, she wasn't always down. After the births of each of our daughters, Julia became strangely exhilarated. She hardly slept, wrote pages of notes. I just figured many mothers get energized that way, and it was a lot better than post-partum blues. Wrong!

When we came home from an exciting vacation, she pushed her enthusiasm, travel stories, and newly gained knowledge of the place on family and friends. I dismissed these episodes as a "lust for life." It seemed cute.

Looking back with the knowledge I have now, I can see that her highs were also responsible for behavior that really upset me. When Julia goes into a high, she's always busy—but accomplishes nearly nothing. She always gets angry at the same people; she's easily distracted. She thinks she's quite creative, yet she creates very little. And she loses track of time. "I'll be ready in five minutes" often means thirty minutes, minimum. If I call her on this, she responds angrily and nastily. She blames other people—especially me—when she mislays something, which, when she gets this way, is often.

It took us twenty-five years to see what was happening: these highs followed long low periods. She had always trivialized her manic moods as "periods of adjustment" after being low for so long. Well, they weren't. Finally, she went through a really scary episode of euphoria that I couldn't ignore. We had her checked out. The diagnosis was bipolar 1.

DUAL DIAGNOSES: COEXISTING PSYCHIATRIC DISORDERS

Often, *dual diagnoses*—the presence of other conditions in addition to bipolar disorder—can complicate the picture. That's because the presence of one psychiatric disorder increases the risk of others. Even doctors can make the mistake of looking for a single ailment and miss the signs of a second condition.

Fortunately, both professionals (who have been keeping track of new information) and the general population (perhaps due to the number of celebrities who are willing to talk publically about their experiences with BD) seem more aware of bipolar disorder today than ever before. Bipolar, once thought to be rare, has been recognized as common, and is less frequently overlooked or misdiagnosed.

Some researchers have estimated that over 70 percent of bipolar patients also have at least one other troubling mental condition. Most common are ADD or ADHD, addictions (including alcoholism), and anxiety disorders (including panic disorder and obsessive-compulsive disorder, also known as OCD). Personality disorders, which are not uncommon in the general population, are also seen in people with BD. Of these, antisocial and borderline personality disorders are most often confused with BD.

Attention Deficit Disorder (ADD)

Perhaps as many as 20 percent of adults with bipolar disorder also have attention deficit disorder (ADD). People who have ADD or ADHD (attention deficit hyperactivity disorder) have difficulty sustaining attention. They are distractible, their minds easily drifting to new topics or thoughts. A person who has ADD may frequently interrupt conversations, even in midsentence, often with information that is not vital or even of particular interest to the listener.

Boys or men with ADHD tend to be especially physically fidgety and overactive, as well as mentally unfocused. In adults, this can show up as the ability to concentrate attention on one or more topics of particular interest to the patient, but impatience and apparent lack of interest in others.

Many of these symptoms are also seen in BD. And many children diagnosed with ADD or ADHD have relatives with BD and later develop BD themselves, suggesting that their attention problems were an early symptom of bipolar disorder. This association has increased concern about medications that are stimulants, which are used for ADD and ADHD but can destabilize mood, especially in people with BD. Careful evaluation and discussion of risks and benefits are essential whenever stimulants are considered for any child or adult with ADD or ADHD—and even more so when there is evidence of BD.

LIVING WITH BD

Christy and Jim

Jim had always had trouble with concentration, and he was in special classes right up through high school. He had been told he had ADD and was tried on stimulants as a child, but they made him irritable. As an adult, he drank a lot of coffee and sometimes took over-the-counter alertness aids to stay focused. He was working on a project on his job that required extra hours and a lot of concentration. He seemed stressed, but I thought he was managing.

Then—it seemed quite suddenly—he went to bed one day and stayed there for more than a week. He slept, maybe, twenty hours a day. I had to force him to eat. He got up to use the

(*continued*)

(*continued*)

bathroom, but that was it. It was really strange, because the week before he had been in such a great mood, talking about how we were going to take a trip around the world, to Europe, Asia, Africa. . . . I was getting really excited about it, and had even started making plans to take a leave of absence from my job. Then he just crashed. He was talking about doing something final, ending the pain. I had no idea what he was talking about, but I was terrified, really.

I called my friend Janet, in tears. She said it reminded her of something that had happened to her dad when she was a teenager, and she asked me if Jim was bipolar. I just said, "What?" I was floored. It had literally never occurred to me.

We live in a really small town, so it's not like we have a lot of psychiatrists. I called my doctor, and she gave me the number of this large hospital in Chicago, a hundred miles away from here. I called, and thank God I did. They helped me figure out how to get him out of bed and into the car, and we drove down to get an evaluation that night. Turns out, he had been taking stimulants from the drugtore to keep up his energy and attention, but had started feeling mood swings. His mood had gotten so bad that he was thinking of suicide. He had to stay in the hospital for a while, but he got a lot better once he started appropriate treatment.

Anxiety

Anxiety disorders, such as generalized anxiety disorder, obsessive-compulsive disorder (OCD), panic disorder, and post-traumatic stress disorder (PTSD), are common in people with bipolar disorder. By some estimates, about 70 percent of people who have BD also suffer from significantly heightened anxiety.

Anxiety is excessive—sometimes obsessive—worry or dread. As any chronic sufferer can tell you, it is exceptionally unpleasant, so much so that the highest rates of suicide are seen in those with anxiety disorders.

An anxious person can be difficult to live with. People who worry a lot can be panicky or morose. They can be short tempered, and may have trouble making decisions or just having fun—or even conceiving of something that *might* be fun.

Sometimes fear and anxiety about consequences can help keep the wilder, more free-wheeling impulses of bipolar disorder in check. More commonly, however, they can make some dangerous symptoms worse. One obvious example is when anxiety prevents someone from seeking needed treatment. And mood swings and anxiety each put an individual at high risk for self-medication (using nonprescription drugs, especially alcohol, to try to relieve symptoms) and suicide.

The good news for the partner of a person who has both BD and an anxiety disorder is that many medications and therapies address both problems simultaneously. Medications for bipolar disorder (we'll discuss these in Chapter Four) can reduce anxiety, and they can be supplemented with cognitive behavioral therapy, relaxation practices, or other treatments that target anxiety.

Occasional use of antianxiety ("anxiolytic") medications (formerly called tranquilizers) can also quell worry. Reducing or eliminating caffeine and other stimulants from the diet (this includes ingredients in some cold and flu preparations) can help lower nervousness. Avoiding these stimulants means carefully reading labels on food and dietary supplements, as well as on over-the-counter medications. Although alcohol can reduce anxiety temporarily, it subsequently causes a rebound and worsening anxiety, along with sleep disruption, in most people. Anxious persons should avoid it, as the short-term relief it offers is not worth its longer-term pain.

Self-Medication and Drug Abuse

Bipolar disorders often lead to "self-medication." This refers to a behavior shared by many people who have mental disorders: using alcohol or illegal drugs, or misusing legitimate medications, to try to reduce agitation or anxiety or to elevate mood in the hope of feeling better.

Unfortunately, this common practice usually just makes things worse and causes symptoms to become less stable over time. An individual with BD who is already feeling lowered inhibitions is all too likely to overindulge in alcohol or illegal drugs. Not surprisingly, this often leads to much bigger problems: more dramatic mood swings, impaired thinking and judgment, addiction.

If your loved one is abusing marijuana, cocaine, alcohol, or other substances, you might take small comfort from knowing that this behavior is far from uncommon and greater comfort from knowing that both bipolar disorder and substance abuse can be treated, often together. It's important to look for signs of drug or alcohol abuse in your partner and to make sure that his or her doctors know about use of any substances, legal or illegal, in addition to prescribed medication.

Antisocial Personality

People with antisocial personality disorder (formerly called sociopathy) lack empathy and can be exceptionally self-centered, manipulative, even unscrupulous, though they are often able to be quite charming. They appear to have a distinct lack of conscience, feel few or no qualms about lying or conniving, and may abuse others verbally and physically. People with BD are probably no more likely than anyone else to be sociopathic; sometimes, however, the two conditions are seen together.

In fact, in several salient ways, they resemble each other. People who are bipolar often appear outgoing, exciting, "life of the party," daring, unfettered by the kinds of worries most adults experience (including, in some instances, fear of the law)—at least when hypomanic. Others often feel drawn to such people. People who have bipolar disorder also can exhibit selfishness, a distinct lack of concern or feeling for others. So can sociopaths.

However, unlike sociopaths, most people with bipolar disorder do tend to care about others and about being honest. An episode of BD may exaggerate self-centeredness and *disinhibition* (that is, a reduction in normal self-control) and lead to inappropriate or dangerous behaviors, including drug use or casual sex. But sociopathy is a lifelong behavior, whereas BD is episodic. In addition, even in the midst of an episode, a person who has only bipolar disorder will still show evidence of conscience. It is likely (given the way the brain works) that BD and sociopathy share some risk factors and brain features, but most people with BD are not sociopathic.

If your partner is violent or abusive, take action. Brutality or abuse caused by BD, substance abuse, or sociopathy is treatable; but treatment is not exactly the same for each, and sociopathy does not respond as well to therapy of any kind. Help your partner get appropriate help, but take care of yourself and your own safety as well.

Borderline Personality

Characterized by unstable self-image and relationships, borderline personality is also typically associated with impulsivity, intense mood swings, anger and irritability, and self-injurious behavior. These latter features are seen in bipolar disorder, as well. However, mood swings in borderline personality tend to be much more rapid than in bipolar disorder and much more reactive to recent experiences or interactions. Thus, unlike bipolar disorder, in which feelings and behavior during episodes of illness are often clearly distinct from feelings and behavior between episodes, people with borderline personality tend to be more reactive to recent or immediate events and more chronically subject to instability of emotion and behavior. Where the two conditions exist together, each can make both the shared symptoms and the symptoms of the other worse, and treatment more difficult. Nonetheless, even together, they do respond to treatment.

COEXISTING MEDICAL DISORDERS

In addition to coexisting psychiatric disorders, a variety of physical illnesses are commonly seen in people with BD. These include heart and blood vessel disease; diabetes mellitus and endocrine diseases at all ages; and neurodegenerative diseases, such as dementia and stroke, in older people with BD. Some medications used to treat BD may, especially by disrupting the handling of fats and sugars, predispose those who have bipolar disorder to these other diseases. However, even taking these treatments into account, there appears to be a higher rate of *comorbidity* (dual diagnoses) between BD and these other illnesses than would be expected by chance alone.

In fact, there is evidence that the association of bipolar disorder with other medical illnesses predates the historical appearance of current treatment for BD. Here again, the reason may be the genes that determine the risk for BD. Their effects can be seen in places other than the brain.

This is even more reason to try to help your partner maintain a good diet and a regular regimen of exercise and sound sleep. These healthful habits will reduce the risk of all the illnesses noted here.

Bipolar People May Need *Help* to Get Help

Why don't people who are bipolar just go get help? Sometimes they do. But more often, they don't recognize they are ill. They may blame someone else for their problems. Or, even if they acknowledge their problems, they may not realize just how much havoc their mood episodes are causing for themselves and those around them. That leaves it up to their loved ones and friends to help the person with BD get help.

The National Institute of Mental Health provides the following information and advice:

- A person with bipolar disorder may need strong encouragement from family and friends to seek treatment. Family physicians can play an important role in providing a referral to a mental health professional.
- Sometimes a family member or friend may need to take the person with bipolar disorder for proper mental health evaluation and treatment.
- A person who is in the midst of a severe episode may need to be hospitalized for his or her own protection and for much-needed treatment. There may be times when the person must be hospitalized against his or her wishes.
- Ongoing encouragement and support are needed after a person obtains treatment, because it may take a while to find the best treatment plan for each individual.
- In some cases, individuals with bipolar disorder may agree, when the disorder is under good control, to a preferred course of action in the event of a future manic or depressive relapse.
- Many people with bipolar disorder benefit from joining support groups such as those sponsored by the National

(continued)

(*continued*)
Depressive and Manic Depressive Association (NDMDA), the National Alliance on Mental Illness (NAMI), and the National Mental Health Association (NMHA). Families and friends can also benefit from support groups offered by these organizations.

WHERE TO GET THE BEST DIAGNOSIS

The best way for your partner to get an accurate diagnosis is to make an appointment with a competent psychiatrist: a medical doctor (MD) with postgraduate training in psychiatry. Some psychiatrists are more experienced with psychotherapies, and some specialize in the diagnosis and treatment of psychiatric disorders, like bipolar disorder, that tend to require medication. They may call themselves "clinical psychopharmacologists," meaning they are experts in the use of drugs to treat mental illness. Psychiatrists tend to see a lot of people with depression and anxiety, because these conditions are so common. Some psychiatrists take a special interest in other psychiatric illnesses and have more experience with them, and you can find psychiatrists who are particularly interested in and knowledgeable about bipolar disorder.

A nonpsychiatrist MD, such as your family doctor, may be able to provide an initial diagnosis. Being MDs, they can also prescribe medication for BD. However, keep in mind that few MDs have much training in psychiatry, and few have the time to treat many people with bipolar disorder. Psychologists and other mental health professionals do not have training in medicine or psychiatry, nor can they prescribe medication in most places. However, they all may play key roles in eventual treatment and may be the first to advise you and your partner to seek a psychiatric evaluation.

Making a Diagnosis

There are no physical tests that can be used to make a diagnosis of bipolar disorder. Rather, bipolar disorder is recognized on the basis of its particular symptoms and the behavior of the patient. A close family member with the illness is also suggestive of a diagnosis of BD. The psychiatrist may obtain blood tests or a brain scan to determine whether some other illness, such as a hormonal disorder or a stroke, has caused symptoms and behaviors similar to those of bipolar disorder. Mostly, however, the psychiatrist will ask questions and observe the patient.

The psychiatrist will ask the patient what he thinks is wrong. She will ask about the patient's mood, thoughts, and activities; about energy, pleasure, worries, and anxieties; about any other illnesses he has; and about any medications or drugs, including prescribed and over-the-counter medications, and legal and illegal drugs, the patient is taking.

The psychiatrist will ask about sleep and appetite. She will ask about memory and concentration, and will ask if the patient is having odd, unusual, rapid, or repetitive thoughts, or thoughts of hurting himself or others. She will ask the patient whether he is having any unusual sensations or perceptions, such as voices heard when no one is speaking. She will ask if anything like what the patient is experiencing now has ever happened before to the patient or to a close relative.

The psychiatrist may refer the patient to a psychologist for testing of thinking—so-called psychological tests—to help clarify exactly what symptoms the patient is having.

Although the patient may be able to provide all the needed information accurately and thoroughly, it is usually helpful for someone else who knows him well and lives with him to participate in the evaluation. Your presence provides support for your loved one and an additional source of information.

This is especially important for bipolar disorder, because BD can affect memory, as well as judgment of what is normal or abnormal. Also, any plans going forward are likely to involve you, as the significant other. The psychiatrist may interview each of you alone as well as together. She may have to keep some things private, but many matters are best addressed if they can be shared.

Your experience with the psychiatrist may be a satisfying and comforting one or may be problematic. An evaluation is always stressful. But if you are not satisfied with the thoroughness of the evaluation, if you do not believe that you were treated well or received the feedback and explanations you needed, or if you and your loved one just don't think you can work with the psychiatrist, you should feel comfortable seeking another opinion and another treatment provider.

For the success of the treatment, it is important that the patient have confidence in the psychiatrist and be comfortable with sharing thoughts and experiences, however abnormal they may be. If you are to be helpful and informed, you will need to have that confidence and comfort, too.

Three Important Questions to Ask Prospective Providers

1. "Are you state licensed?" (The only acceptable answer is "Yes.")
2. "About how long would you expect the evaluation and treatment to take?" Most therapists won't be able to answer precisely before talking with the prospective patient, but it's wise to try to get an idea.
3. "How much clinical experience do you have treating patients who have bipolar disorder?" Generally speaking, the more experience, the greater the likelihood of success.

FINDING A PSYCHIATRIST

A good place to begin your search for a psychiatrist who is familiar with treating bipolar disorder is your local psychiatric or teaching hospital or mental health facility, or one in the nearest large city. Universities and their medical centers often have affiliated programs. Your primary care physician will probably be able to help with a referral. There is a wealth of information available on the Internet, where you can search for specialists of any kind, many of whose credentials and training are listed. The local branch of the American Psychiatric Association will have information on qualified psychiatrists. Your HMO should also be able to provide a list of its preferred providers.

As with a search for any kind of doctor, personal recommendations can be valuable. Word-of-mouth recommendations can be helpful if you have friends or family in your geographic area who have benefited from psychiatric care and are willing to share information. Your clergyperson, local hospital, or a bipolar support group could all be good places to begin your search.

The Depression and Bipolar Support Alliance (DBSA; 800-826-3632; DBSAlliance.org) maintains a database of patient-recommended professionals as well as providers categorized by insurance coverage they accept. The National Alliance on Mental Illness, NAMI (800-950-NAMI/6264; NAMI.org), lists resources for finding mental health professionals and free or low-cost health care and medication. The Web site of the Mood and Anxiety Disorders Institute of Massachusetts General Hospital, www2.massgeneral.org/madi resourcecenter/sitemap.asp, lists a page of resources, not limited to that state, for finding therapists. The publisher Castle Connolly puts out reference books and maintains a Web site listing well-regarded medical doctors, organized by geographic region and field of specialization. To find a psychiatrist, you can search through the company's books in most libraries or order your own (about $25 to $30 a copy). The publisher also maintains a Web site database you can search for about $10 a day or $25 a year. A free option offers limited searching. Keep in mind that doctors are nominated by peers, so don't discount other psychiatric professionals who might be just as good, but not as popular and therefore less likely to be included.

Get information from more than one source before you decide on a psychiatrist.

HEALTH INSURANCE

If your partner is willing and able to share the responsibility of finding a good psychiatrist or psychotherapist, so much the better. If not, you'll need to start the ball rolling yourself.

If your partner has mental health coverage or an employee assistance program (EAP) through his job, refer to that first. If you don't know the details of the coverage, contact the human resources department at work.

If your partner has private health coverage, contact the insurance company directly. Your partner's insurance company should be able to recommend qualified providers who accept its coverage. Don't feel afraid to call. In some states, it is incumbent on insurance companies to provide coverage for appropriate treatment.

You might need to make repeated calls until you find a representative who can give you the information you need. Be persistent. Most insurance companies also have Web sites that may be helpful.

If You Can't Afford Treatment

Psychiatric care can be expensive. Some degree of coverage for psychiatric care is mandated by law. Not only private insurance but also Medicare and Medicaid both provide coverage for psychiatric evaluation and treatment. If you do not have insurance, you can explore several options for lower-cost care. If the symptoms of illness are disabling, a patient may be eligible for public insurance coverage.

Many communities have nonprofit counseling or psychiatric clinics. Some mental health professionals work on a sliding scale: payment according to income. This information may not be offered if you don't ask. A doctor who does not offer this option might be able to refer you to one who does. Some doctors and hospitals may be willing to negotiate cost.

Government mental health clinics and medical health clinics that offer behavioral health services are a good source of low-cost care. Look in the government listings ("blue pages") section of your local telephone directory for the state offices of mental health.

You can also call the SAMHSA, the U.S. Substance Abuse & Mental Health Services Administration (800-662-HELP) for referrals and information. Know that any of these options could mean a longer-than-average wait for appointment times, as resources are usually stretched thin.

Once your partner has received a thorough evaluation and diagnosis, you, your spouse, and the doctor can plan a course of treatment. In most cases, that will include mood stabilizers and other medication in conjunction with psychosocial treatments, such as cognitive behavioral therapy, family therapy, and others we will discuss in Chapter Five. As we'll see in the next chapter, however, stabilizing mood through medication is generally a priority.

CHAPTER 4

Understanding Medication

I'm fine, but I'm bipolar. I'm on seven medications, and I take medication three times a day. This constantly puts me in touch with the illness I have. I'm never quite allowed to be free of that for a day. It's like being a diabetic.

—Carrie Fisher, actress and author

Medication does not "cure" bipolar disorder. But it can markedly reduce the frequency and severity of mood swings. Sometimes extreme moods and other symptoms break through despite the medication. These, too, can be treated with more or different medication. People with BD, like people with any illness, often resist the idea of medication. Even if they know they need treatment, they are fearful that possible side effects will be worse than living with the disorder itself. The risks and discomforts of drug treatment are real, but so are the risks and discomforts of untreated illness. When symptoms of BD are disrupting or threatening life, medication is the first and most effective choice for treatment, and will help your partner to live a more stable life.

It's likely that your partner will end up trying several medications, dosages, or even drug combinations before arriving at the one that best manages the symptoms with a minimum of side effects. This regimen will probably continue to help for many years. However, even after an effective treatment regimen has been found, continued regular checkups and adjustments over time will be critical to maintaining a good balance between beneficial effects and side effects of medication.

COMMONLY PRESCRIBED MEDICATIONS FOR BIPOLAR DISORDER

Your partner's doctor will have a number of drugs to choose from. Many of the older drugs, like lithium, are still around, and they still work. New medications are approved each year, and new developments can make older medications more effective or less toxic. Although newer medications are often preferred because of better effects or lower incidences of side effects, they won't work for everyone.

No one medication is a panacea for BD's symptoms, and they are often prescribed in combination. Here's a brief description of medications you and your partner might encounter in treatment under a doctor's prescription. Please keep in mind that everyone is a little different and that each of these medications, even those that don't help most patients, may help *some* people with bipolar disorder.

Lithium

Lithium—the first mood-stabilizing medication approved by the U.S. Food and Drug Administration (FDA) for treatment of mania—is the medication with the longest history when it comes to treating mental illness (see Chapter Two). It can be very effective in preventing the recurrence of both manic and depressive episodes.

People who use lithium must go in for regular blood tests and take the medication consistently, often on a strict schedule, because lithium levels must be maintained within a relatively narrow range to achieve beneficial effects while avoiding toxic effects. Also, to help keep lithium levels in the right range, patients must take care to avoid dehydration or excess salt loss. Despite these inconveniences, many patients who follow this regimen are well rewarded with an impressive reduction in bipolar symptoms.

Potential side effects include, rarely, kidney disorders, which the blood tests help detect before problems start. The more common side effects are increased thirst, water retention, and urination. Lithium can also cause tremor, stomach upset, diarrhea, nausea, vomiting, and, at high levels, confusion. Sometimes lithium will reduce the functioning of the thyroid gland; this too is monitored by blood tests and can be treated.

Many of these side effects can be mitigated with changes in dosage or the addition of other medications. However, you and your partner must be aware of the consequences of trying to treat the side effects with other drugs. For example, patients who take diuretics along with lithium could be headed for serious medical trouble if the lithium dosage is not carefully adjusted. A number of other medicines, including common pain relievers, can also interact badly with lithium. Always consult your doctor or pharmacist before taking *any* additional medication.

Many patients feel daunted by lithium's reputation for serious side effects. But many others benefit greatly from its use. Keep in mind, too, that typical dosages today are lower than they were years ago, and that different forms of the medication may reduce side effects. Recent reviews have suggested that lithium is underutilized in the treatment of BD due to its reputation for side effects, the need for blood level monitoring, and competition from newer, aggressively advertised drugs. No medication has been shown to be better than lithium in the treatment of BD. Properly used, it is often not only well tolerated and effective, but also more affordable than other medications.

 ## LIVING WITH BD

Ted and Keisha

In our bipolar support group, I hear lots of stories about people's bad experiences with lithium. One guy said he had nonstop diarrhea. A woman said she stopped because her hair started falling out. Another woman said her appetite came back and she gained too much weight . . . it went on and on.

So after hearing all this, my wife, Keisha, was terrified when her doctor prescribed lithium. But she's been taking it for a few months now, and other than the basic hassles of being on medication—keeping to a schedule, which is hard for her, and having to get regular blood tests, which I help make sure she does—her only complaint is being thirsty all the time and having to find restrooms when she's out. It's a tradeoff we can deal with.

Mood-Stabilizing Anticonvulsants

There's good evidence that several anticonvulsant medications are effective against BD. These include valproic acid, also called valproate, and the related divalproex (Depakene® and Depakote®), lamotrigene (Lamictal®), and carbamazepine (Tegretol®). Gabapentin (Neurontin®), topiramate

(Topamax®), and other anticonvulsants are also sometimes prescribed, although there is less evidence of their efficacy.

Valproate (Depakote) seems most effective against mania and also to stabilize mood. Lamotrigene (Lamictal) appears effective against bipolar depression. It carries a low but not insignificant risk of a life-threatening condition called Stevens-Johnson syndrome, which is marked by high fever, followed by mucous membrane irritation and a spreading, blistering rash. Other rashes are also not uncommon with lamotrigene. Starting at a low dose and gradually increasing it seems to be the key to preventing serious side effects.

As is true of any medication, careful observation is important—especially when beginning the prescription or after a dosage increase. Any rash or fever should be reported promptly to your doctor.

There is currently some dispute as to how effective lamotrigene is and whether it can increase the risk of mania. It may be most effective for bipolar 2 disorder. The matching of drugs to patients has not been well worked out, and best treatment is often found by trial and error. Nonetheless, a great many patients have appeared to benefit from lamotrigene and other anticonvulsant drugs, and many more will continue to do so.

Anticonvulsants are often combined with lithium, or with other anticonvulsants, to achieve enhanced effects. Increased side effects must also be watched for in anyone combining multiple medications.

Antipsychotic Drugs

Antipsychotic medications are most closely associated with the treatment of brain disorders like schizophrenia, but they are also effective for mania. They treat both manic symptoms and psychotic ones that occur with mania or depression.

The most commonly used older, so-called typical anti-psychotic is haloperidol (Haldol®). Some—especially the newer, so-called atypical antipsychotics, as well as clozapine (Clozaril®), the drug on which these atypicals were mod-eled—may have some degree of antidepressant or mood-sta-bilizing effects.

The new class of antipsychotics is called atypical because these drugs are less likely to produce the typical side effects of the older antipsychotics: tremor, stiffness, or muscle spasm. The atypicals include risperidone (Risperdal®), olanzapine (Zyprexa®), quetiapine (Seroquel®), ziprasidone (Geodon®), aripiprazole (Abilify®), paliperidone (Invega®), iloperidone (Fanapt®), and asenapine (Saphris®). All present similar therapeutic effects but different side effects—notably, differ-ent degrees of stimulation or sedation (that is, wakefulness, even agitation, or sleepiness). Some, especially olanzapine and clozapine, are more likely to cause weight gain, elevated blood lipids, and a risk of diabetes mellitus. Clozapine sometimes works better than other antipsychotic drugs, but it also has the most side effects. Rarely, clozapine causes a dramatic and potentially life-threatening reduction in the production of white blood cells—needed to protect the body from infection. So using clozapine means getting regular blood tests.

As of this writing, several other atypical antipsychotic drugs are under evaluation for approval by the FDA (the U.S. Government Food and Drug Administration). Most of the drugs under development have properties very similar to drugs already on the market, but a few are quite different and may have new and useful effects. Your doctor is your best source of information on the availability of new treatments. You can always check online, including going to the FDA Web site (www.fda.gov), to see what is being said about new and currently approved drugs.

Antidepressants

In many cases, doctors prescribe medications approved and commonly used for depression. These include selective serotonin reuptake inhibitors (SSRIs), serotonin and norepinephrine reuptake inhibitors (SNRIs), monoamine oxidase inhibitors (MAOIs), or tricyclic antidepressants (TCAs), and a few others that don't fit these classifications.

The use of antidepressants in patients with bipolar disorder is currently controversial. All of the antidepressants were developed for and tested in major or unipolar depression, not the depression of bipolar disorder. Some experts say they don't work for depression in BD; others say they can induce mania. Practically speaking, as depression is common in those with BD, antidepressants are often prescribed. They probably work best in concert with mood-stabilizing medication. They are rarely used alone in BD. Among them are the following.

SSRIs

SSRIs, such as fluoxetine (better known under the name Prozac®), are frequently prescribed for bipolar, depression, but there is debate about whether they can induce mania or rapid cycling in some patients. All antidepressants, including SSRIs, have been known to induce agitation in some bipolar, as well as nonbipolar, patients. However, they can probably help other patients with bipolar depression and are used when depression is disabling and unremitting.

SSRIs were developed, in part, as an alternative to the older TCAs (tricyclic antidepressants), which were effective but tended to have a lot of side effects (such as dry mouth, blurred vision, lightheadedness, and sedation). The SSRIs did elevate mood without most of these side effects, but they have side effects of their own, such as the aforementioned agitation.

They also reduce sexual performance, especially in some men, by reducing the strength of erections and inhibiting ejaculation and orgasm. Like all side effects, these unwanted consequences may fade with time and treatment. However, they are matters that should be discussed between partners. The prescribing doctor should also be told of any side effects, especially as they are the most common reason people don't take their medication.

In addition to Prozac, SSRIs include sertraline (Zoloft®), citalopram (Celexa®), escitalopram (Lexapro®), fluvoxamine (Luvox®), and paroxetine (Paxil®). SSRIs primarily affect serotonin, a molecule used as a chemical signal between cells in the brain.

SNRIs

SNRIs also work on serotonin, but, especially at higher doses, they work on the chemical signal norepinephrine, too, to try to achieve a greater effect. Note, however, that no one antidepressant has consistently proven more effective than the others. In addition, remember that most comparisons of antidepressants have been made among patients with major (unipolar) depression, not patients with bipolar depression.

Examples of SNRIs include venlafaxine (Effexor®), duloxetine (Cymbalta®), and desvenlafaxine (Pristiq®).

MAOIs

MAOIs were the first-discovered class of antidepressant medication. They are not usually the first drugs prescribed, in part because they carry dietary restrictions and can cause large drops or rises in blood pressure. However, they sometimes work where other medications have failed. It's all a matter of finding the right prescription for your unique partner.

A person using MAOIs must avoid many different foods and even beverages, especially fermented or aged ones, including cheeses, aged meats, pickled foods, and red wine. MAOIs, like most medications, are known to interact with certain other medicines and even over-the-counter preparations, especially cold medication. MAOIs include isocarboxazid (Marplan®), phenelzine (Nardil®), tranylcypromine (Parnate®), and selegiline (Emsam®).

TCAs

Tricyclic antidepressants (TCAs) are another older class of medication. Elavil®—generically, amitriptyline—is perhaps the best known, along with imipramine, originally marketed as Tofranil®. Like MAOIs, they are generally not the first treatment considered for bipolar disorder. Like all antidepressants, they can cause agitation or stimulation and may aggravate mania.

Wellbutrin®

Wellbutrin (bupropion hydrochloride) is neither an SSRI, SNRI, MAOI, nor a TCA. It is an antidepressant sometimes used to treat bipolar disorder. (Its classification, in case you're wondering, is aminoketone.)

Wellbutrin (generically, bupropion) is not recommended for people who have epilepsy or who have been diagnosed with eating disorders, because such patients are thought to have a higher risk of seizures. Neither is it recommended for patients taking Zyban® sustained-release tablets, because they also contain bupropion, or for those using MAOIs or nicotine patches. Other medications can also cause interactions.

Unhappily, Wellbutrin is less likely to alleviate depression than other antidepressants. On the plus side, it's said to produce fewer sexual side effects than the commonly used SSRIs and less weight gain than some of the other medications. Also, there is some evidence that it is less likely than other antidepressants to induce mania.

Mirtazapine

Mirtazapine (Remeron®) is another antidepressant in its own class. It seems to work through certain receptors (called alpha 2 receptors) for norepinephrine along with certain receptors for serotonin. It is very sedating and can cause appetite increase with weight gain, but is an effective, approved antidepressant.

Compounding Pharmacies for Drug Sensitivities and Other Needs

Compounding pharmacies (including some but not all drug stores) can formulate medication to fit the specific needs of a patient. If your partner has sensitivities or requires unconventional dosages, a compounding pharmacy may be the way to go.

For example, if your partner is taking medication that provokes or exacerbates allergies or other sensitivities, compounding pharmacies can make prescriptions without dyes or other ingredients, or formulate liquid or (sometimes) transdermal patch forms of medications normally available only as pills. They can also make extra-low-dosage pills.

It is often easier to make patch forms of older medications, because those are more likely to be available in powder form. Compounding pharmacies can also make medications in suppository form, though this option is more popular in Europe than the United States. This method allows for lower dosages, because the medication is absorbed more directly into the bloodstream, rather than through the entire digestive tract.

To locate a compounding pharmacy, visit the International Association of Compounding Pharmacies: http://www.iacprx.org/, call (281) 933-8400, or inquire at your regular pharmacy. Some large cities have more than one.

NONCOMPLIANCE

Noncompliance—not taking prescribed medication as directed—is one of the most troubling problems in treating all illnesses. If a patient doesn't take the drug on the correct schedule, stops and starts the drug independently, or stops taking it altogether, the drug will not perform as it should, may lead to worsening rather than relief of symptoms, and may produce more intense side effects—in some cases, even life-threatening side effects.

Bipolar patients are no exception when it comes to noncompliance. Except in very specific situations requiring use of the legal system, an adult cannot be forced into taking medication or accepting any other treatment. If your partner does not take prescribed medication, or does not take it as prescribed, you may feel frustrated or angry, and your partner may feel more ill than is necessary.

Although many patients are eager for help and diligent about symptom management, more often than not, people don't take medication as prescribed. There are many reasons your bipolar partner might stop taking medication or feel fearful or reluctant to start:

- In some cases, a prescription may cause unpleasant or embarrassing side effects, or threaten to. Indeed, the reputations of some medications precede them.
- Some patients feel creative and happy when manic, and are reluctant to lose those feelings. Others feel so good once their symptoms are medicated that they can hardly believe they'll be troubled again by mental illness—so they simply stop their meds. They're usually wrong, and symptoms return.
- Still others have difficulty remembering schedules or sticking to them.

- Some patients feel depressed just *thinking* about being "on medication" for life.
- Medication can be frightening, and with good reason. Even medicine that makes life livable where it once was not can later be found to cause harm.

It's not unlikely that only one of you wants to see your partner on medication! Try to summon up your sympathy about resistance while remaining firm that it must be overcome.

 LIVING WITH BD

Virginia and Ty

Right from the start, Ty *hated* taking medication. I think that's because the first time, before his more accurate diagnosis of bipolar disorder, he was treated with a prescription for depression—and that sent him into a wild manic episode. After being practically catatonic before the meds, he literally did not sleep for three days. He just paced around the house naked. Very scary for me.

When he was finally diagnosed bipolar, I think we were both relieved—that made sense to us. But the idea of having to take pills every day did not sit well at all. I held the line, though—I told him that if he wasn't going to do what he needed to take care of himself, I was leaving. I'd help him in any way possible, but he had to do this. So he does take his meds, but it's been a real struggle for him.

At one point over the years, his doctor had him on lithium and five other meds to control his BD. It seemed like every time he had an attack, the doc just added another drug. Doctor Jarvis is a good guy, and we trust him, but you just didn't know whether to laugh or cry when confronted with that lineup of pill bottles in the bathroom!

Sometimes Ty grumbles that he just doesn't feel like himself on medication. Like, he's not ticklish anymore, for one thing. I know for a fact he misses the exhilaration of being manic. I don't miss that at all. The side effects have gotten more tolerable over the years. And neither of us misses those dark depressions! I'm glad we stuck with treatment, and on the whole, Ty is, too.

CHANGING MEDICATION

If your partner is at least willing to *try* different prescribed medications, that's good. However, as you may already know, it can prove harrowing for both of you. If, for instance, your partner has had unpleasant side effects, or if your partner is frustrated and wants to swear off meds for good, then what?

Well, two things: a partner who's reluctant to give medication a try can be persuaded. We're not saying it's easy, only that it's possible. Remind your partner that a trial is just that, a trial—it doesn't necessarily mean a lifelong commitment.

If your partner hasn't found the right medication, drug combination, or dosage, work with your provider—or, if necessary, find another one. Waiting for results can be frustrating indeed, and drugs can take weeks or months to adjust and more weeks or months to work, but patience is often rewarded.

If treatment isn't going well, it's always all right, and usually wise, to ask for a reevaluation or consultation. Good doctors know they don't know everything and can benefit from another look and advice. Don't feel afraid to ask. If your doctor opposes a consultation, think about finding a new provider.

TAKING MEDICATION SAFELY

According to numerous studies, medication, though imperfect, has proven remarkably effective in helping manage the symptoms of bipolar disorder. Nevertheless, supporting your partner through various medication trials with their side effects can feel demoralizing, exhausting, or even frightening. Try to see the psychiatrist or psychopharmacologist together. If possible, talk with your partner and write down questions ahead of time. Write down the advice you get, too, to help you remember how to use the medication correctly so that you can monitor your partner.

You should both keep in mind the following information as you begin considering and using any medication recommended by your doctor.

Monitor Side Effects

Any medication can cause side effects—that is, a drug might treat one problem, but cause others. Usually the problems caused are milder than the ones solved, but that is not always so.

Almost always, medications used to treat BD must build up in the body and be present for days or weeks at an effective level before there's a substantial improvement in symptoms. They don't work directly and immediately to treat BD. However, side effects often appear immediately—long before the medicine begins to work successfully on the symptoms it's being used to treat. So you both might need extra patience when assessing whether the medication will help.

Many side effects are easily tolerated or offset. For example, a dry mouth caused by medication can be alleviated by drinking water or sucking on a hard candy (sugarless is important, as a dry mouth can increase the risk of cavities).

Some side effects, however, may be more difficult to deal with. If a medication causes vomiting, for instance, or a rash or tremor, or confusion, contact the prescribing doctor immediately. In many cases, the dosage can be adjusted but the medication may need to be stopped. Still, make sure to check with the doctor before discontinuing any medication, as there may be withdrawal effects.

Beware of Nutritional and Herbal Supplements for BD

At some point in your search for treatment, you may hear about dietary and herbal supplements to treat bipolar disorder or depression. Maintaining a healthy, balanced diet is important for everyone, and certainly important for those with BD, who are at increased risk for various medical illnesses and whose illness may affect their appetite and choice of food. However, *there is no good evidence that additional supplementation with vitamins, minerals, or other dietary constituents is useful in BD.*

Omega 3 fatty acids have been shown in some studies to help with unipolar depression, but the evidence in bipolar depression is weak, at best. Remember, when you are using dietary constituents to treat illness, you are using them in higher than normal amounts—as drugs, not food. Their safety as drugs has not been tested, and is usually not known.

Herbal supplements are even more problematic. You may hear, particularly, about St. John's wort (Hypericum perforatum). Herbal preparations like St. John's wort are not tested for safety, effectiveness, or even for actual ingredients. It is difficult to know what you are getting when you buy them. Sometimes these supplements have no effects, but they are not necessarily inactive. They may also have effects quite different or even opposite to the ones you seek. No one knows.

One very important point to note arises from the way they are often sold: as "natural." This makes them sound pleasant and wholesome, but they may not be. In particular, they are not necessarily safe because they are natural. Many toxic and dangerous herbs and foods are natural.

Avoid (or at Least Discuss) Drug Combinations

To reduce the possibility of negative interactions, each of your partner's doctors—psychiatrist, general practitioner, and others—should be made aware of *all* medications your partner is taking. This includes common over-the-counter preparations (those purchased without prescription) for colds, allergies, pain relief, stomach upset, dietary supplementation, or anything else. It also includes herbal remedies, supplements, and alternative medicine.

Take Special Care with Medications During Pregnancy

Pregnancy can exacerbate, or even initiate, bipolar symptoms. Pregnant women, or those who may become pregnant, need to take special care with all medications to protect themselves and their babies.

Although many of the medications prescribed for BD are relatively safe, others are more dangerous to a developing fetus. With a planned pregnancy, the relative risks of stopping or continuing individual medications should be discussed ahead of time with the treating psychiatrist and, if recommended, with an expert who specializes in drug use during pregnancy. For an unplanned pregnancy, a discussion with the treating psychiatrist and, if needed, consultation with a specialist should be arranged as early as possible. Some pregnant women choose to try to go through pregnancy without any medication, but stopping medication can lead to an exacerbation of illness and even the need to take more medication(s) than would otherwise have been necessary.

At a minimum, there should be a well-considered plan for how to monitor and treat symptoms during pregnancy. Although most medications do not appear at high levels in breast milk, caution is also needed for women who are nursing, so that the baby is not unnecessarily exposed to medication. Nursing while on medication should be discussed with your doctor.

If your partner is pregnant, or contemplating becoming pregnant, and she is taking medication for BD, make sure to inform her gynecologist and general practitioner, and make sure these doctors and the treating psychiatrist are in contact with one another.

Understand the Medication

Ask your doctor or pharmacist to explain any terms you do not understand in relation to the drugs your partner is taking. For example, the comment "This medicine has a long [or short] half-life" refers to how long a medication remains in the body. It is so named because it actually measures how long it takes for *half* of the medication to be eliminated from the body after it is absorbed.

In general, it takes over five times the half-life for a new dose of medication to build up to its maximal level. Thus, if a drug has a half-life of twenty-four hours, it will be over five days of taking the drug daily before the level of the drug has hit its peak. Similarly, if a medication is stopped, it doesn't just disappear. It can take many times the half-life for enough of the drug to leave the system so that most or all of its effects, especially side effects, disappear.

Don't Stop Suddenly

Suddenly stopping effective medication can be dangerous. Symptoms can return quickly and increase dramatically, and there can be other dangerous effects of withdrawal. In most cases, getting off a medication, like starting medication, needs to be done gradually and under the supervision of your physician.

It is not *always* necessary to gradually decrease dosages of a drug that is causing a bad reaction. For example, if a medicine has just recently been started, the patient can usually simply stop taking it. Nonetheless, this is not a decision your partner can make. *Always* consult the prescribing doctor or pharmacist before making any major decision regarding medication.

Although medication is helpful for millions of patients, it's not ideal for everyone. Your partner might, for example, be unable to tolerate side effects or find the right medication, combination, or dosage—or, like many patients, refuse even to try it. Or your partner may be pregnant, and wish to avoid medication, if possible, as medication might harm her baby. Or the medicine might help, but not diminish symptoms completely. If any of these situations is so for you, take heart. In the next chapter, we will look at other treatment options that can be used in conjunction with medication, or alone.

CHAPTER 5

Understanding Psychosocial Therapies and Medical Treatment Options

Get counseling or therapy for everyone in the family, not just the "sick" kid. No one ever wants to take this advice, but it's incredibly important.
—Lizzie Simon, My *Bipolar Road Trip in 4-D*

Your partner's psychiatrist, along with prescribing medication, will schedule regular appointments to monitor progress. At those meetings, the doctor will review the medications your partner is taking and will assess both beneficial and side effects. Most psychiatrists will also discuss how other aspects of life are going and help with choices and problem solving; this is often called "supportive therapy." The best bet for optimally effective treatment, however, often includes some additional kind of formal psychotherapy ("talk" therapy) in combination with a primary medical therapy. That is, although the primary treatment is most likely to be medication, a thorough approach to an illness that affects thinking, feeling, and behavior will usually include one of the therapies designed to address psychological and social issues. The treating psychiatrist may provide this therapy, or may focus on the medical treatment and refer the patient to an expert in psychosocial therapies for additional care.

Although therapy is primarily for the bipolar patient, it often includes family or couples therapy with the person's partner. Support groups for both members of the couple (discussed in Chapter Six) are also often helpful. Many patients and their partners, faced with the already daunting task of managing and paying for daily medication, wonder why they should add additional hours simply talking.

First, it's important to note that psychotherapies are not "simply talking." They address each individual person's particular problems and help find different and healthier ways of thinking and acting. A lot of psychotherapy for BD deals in practical solutions, along with helping the patient regulate and improve feelings. Studies show that forms of psychotherapy designed to fit the needs of bipolar patients, in combination with medication, can be more effective for mood stabilization and daily functioning than medication alone. Most can be used for short periods of time, at the beginning of treatment and when new problems arise, so they do not necessarily require an extreme commitment of time and money.

PSYCHOSOCIAL THERAPY OPTIONS

Several psychotherapy options seem to be effective for the individual with BD, including cognitive-behavioral therapy, dialectical behavioral therapy, and interpersonal social rhythm therapy. Some of these approaches can help a spouse or partner, too. Family therapy or couples counseling can also be of great help in identifying and addressing problems in a relationship. For the best results, follow the specific treatment plan designed by your partner's treating doctor.

Cognitive-Behavioral Therapy (CBT)

Cognitive-behavioral therapy (sometimes called simply "behavioral therapy") combines its two approaches—cognitive and behavioral—to help patients identify and confront less-than-helpful ways of thinking, false or inaccurate beliefs, and exaggerated or unfounded fears. (You may also encounter a therapy called REBT, rational emotive behavior therapy, sometimes just called rational therapy. This precursor to CBT seeks to help patients evaluate the degree of rationality in their thoughts. For example, do we feel bad because of things that happen or because of the way we *perceive* these events? This question from REBT is the foundation of all cognitive-behavioral therapies.)

Cognitive therapies deal with modes of thinking and target practical ways to improve thoughts and mood. Depressed patients, for example, sometimes experience what are known as automatic thoughts—habitual ideas that have become ingrained ("I am worthless," "Everyone always leaves me," and so on). In such cases, the therapist might ask the patient to realistically evaluate whether her life is really as bleak as she believes; whether she is, in fact, worthless; and so on. Usually there is contrary evidence to these extreme views. The patient and therapist then explore and practice other ways to see things.

In some cases, the patient might be asked to explore the potential result of an obsessive fear coming true: "What would happen if you *did* lose your job?" "How *would* you deal with a burglary at your house?" This sort of realistic exploration helps defuse fears and allows patients to at least contemplate taking positive action.

In the case of extreme anxiety, an active cognitive-behavioral component would likely come into play. The therapist might, for example, direct the patient to describe her worries in detail, imagining fears coming true. Examined closely, these beliefs usually turn out to be excessive, or it becomes clear that they could be handled. For example, the patient may realize after assessment that the likelihood of losing her job is small and that she would have good options even if that happened. She might also realize that there are practical things she should do to insure her continued employment or to plan for change. Rethinking issues and taking action are frequently helpful not only for mood but also to make sure we are doing everything we can to enhance our life and opportunities.

In addition, working at the juncture of thought and behavior, the patient might learn techniques—including controlled breathing, muscle relaxation, yoga, and other physical methods—to learn to achieve a calmer state and apply that learning to reduce overactive responses to stressful thoughts or situations. The patient might learn other methods that, like relaxation exercises, arise from a long tradition of studies of meditation to reduce unwanted or harmful thoughts and increase helpful thinking. Healthier thinking leads to healthier feeling and activities. That leads to the behavioral side of CBT.

As you can already see, the cognitive and the behavioral are intimately interwoven. Healthier thinking and feeling, the effects of cognitive therapy, will allow the patient to engage in healthier behavior, with healthier choices of activities and interactions. Similarly, in addition to learning to think in more productive and appropriate ways, the patient may work, through behavioral therapy, to create a better lifestyle, with healthier activities and relationships. Just as healthier thinking can lead to healthier behavior, healthier behavior can lead to better experiences, better feelings, and better thoughts. Thus the two halves of cognitive-behavioral therapy use the interacting sides of our dual nature as emotional and physical beings to improve our feelings and choices.

Cognitive-behavioral therapy was developed, in part, for patients with anxiety disorders, such as obsessive-compulsive disorder (OCD), panic disorder, and social phobias. As we saw earlier, many bipolar patients have a dual diagnosis of anxiety disorder, and in that case, CBT can be especially helpful. The treatment of OCD provides a good example of the use of CBT. In this anxiety disorder, worries torment the patient to the degree that he feels driven to do anything he can to prevent them from returning. Usually he develops associated behaviors to help reduce anxiety—called *compulsions* because the person feels compelled to perform them. A germ-phobic person, for example, may wash his hands hundreds of time per day in hopes of warding off dangerous pathogens.

Cognitive-behavioral therapists work with patients to gradually confront long-held terrors and unlearn or reduce habitual thoughts and behaviors, often through the use of "homework" exercises. A patient may be able to unlearn repetitive hand washing by redirecting his thinking and practicing new actions. As another example, using the technique known as exposure therapy, the therapist might ask a person with a social phobia (excessive fear of social situations)—a very common type of anxiety disorder—to practice being in social situations in the therapist's office, to apply relaxation techniques to remain calm, and to slowly work up to being able to attend and enjoy real, unpracticed social situations.

The methods of CBT are useful for many psychiatric disorders, not just for anxiety. They can be applied for symptoms of bipolar disorder, schizophrenia, and other severe psychiatric disorders, such as low mood, poor concentration, and impulsivity. And CBT does work. Several studies have demonstrated its effectiveness, and anecdotal evidence is strong.

One useful application of CBT is to assist the patient in achieving compliance with prescribed treatment, medication in particular. For example, the patient may feel that "only weak people take medications" or that "the medications are addictive." These are incorrect assessments. The therapist can explore these thoughts and their rationales with the patient. The patient learns to identify, challenge, and change such thoughts and replace them with healthier thinking. This approach can be applied to any aspect of treatment the patient may reject out of misunderstanding, misconception, or misapprehension.

Cognitive-behavioral therapy has two important benefits. First, its gains are believed to be long lasting. That's rarely true of medication, which will stop working soon after one stops taking it. And second, it's almost never harmful. Unlike medication, it has no physical side effects. It won't be taken off the market.

 ## LIVING WITH BD

Leo and Cara

I have to give my wife a lot of credit—Cara hung in for a really long time, trying new medication combinations, until her doc finally found the one that seemed to do the trick. He put her on four different kinds of pills, and—miracle of miracles!—they worked. I had to help her keep on track with the meds, and keep her appointments, but finally her moods stabilized. I was so proud of her.

Unfortunately, Cara wasn't quite ready to celebrate. She'd been so traumatized by her early experiences—she struggled with wild mood swings for years before she was diagnosed, and got herself into some dangerous situations—that she couldn't accept the meds were really working. Plus, her boss kept calling and asking when she was coming back to work— she's a contract attorney, really good at what she does. Of course her boss knew that she wasn't going to work on cases around the clock for days anymore, but she was still a valuable employee. Cara really wanted to go back to work, too. But she was also freaking out—she just didn't believe she had the skills to cope anymore. It was like she had to learn a whole new way of being at work, engaging with people, focusing on details . . .

Her doc told her she needed to get back on the horse, and suggested seeing someone for cognitive-behavioral therapy. When he explained what it was, I thought it sounded perfect—working on changing her negative thought patterns, working on time management, even some relaxation techniques . . . hey, who couldn't use some CBT in their lives?

There were some tears as she struggled with the idea—change is scary for everybody, I told her. But she'd made *so* much progress, and she didn't want to stop. She wanted to keep moving forward. So she went to this psychologist, a woman this time, which also appealed to her. And it worked! She's back at work, and she's functioning much better than she ever has. She's even learned some new tricks that help her keep on top of her med schedule so *I* can relax a little too!

Dialectical Behavior Therapy (DBT)

Dialectical behavior therapy is a relatively new therapy developed, in part, to assist emotional regulation in patients with borderline personality disorder. Although it is still most commonly associated with that condition, dialectical behavior therapy has shown promise for treating mood swings in anxious, depressed, and bipolar patients as well.

Dialectical behavior therapy blends cognitive and behavioral therapy techniques to assess alternative ways of thinking and behaving and to change what is changeable, with Zen principles of accepting ourselves and our lives. Like CBT, from which it derives, it relies on homework exercises to help patients learn healthier ways of thinking and feeling. A full course of DBT usually requires commitment to weekly group and individual therapy for an extended time, about one year. Although DBT is not commonly used for bipolar disorder, elements from DBT, such as a focus on learning mood regulation and working on social skills, may be used in CBT to treat someone with BD.

Interpersonal Therapy

Interpersonal therapy is quite effective in addressing relationship problems. Although it is used more typically for depression, it can also be helpful for people who have bipolar disorder. The interactions between the therapist and patient in the session are used to illuminate the patient's interactions in general. The therapist and patient also discuss how the patient is thinking and feeling about and handling other relationships, and they discuss other ways to think about and live in those relationships.

This therapy focuses mainly on the individual's current conflicts and relationships, rather than past experiences. This is usually a short-term treatment, lasting for about twenty one-hour sessions over about as many weeks.

Interpersonal Social Rhythm Therapy (IPSRT)

Interpersonal social rhythm therapy (IPSRT) was designed specifically for bipolar disorder, and has the advantage of addressing it in three important ways: helping with monitoring thinking, feeling, and relationships; addressing practical problems that arise; and maintaining regular rhythms of daily activity, eating, and sleeping. This therapy is fairly new and is not yet widely practiced, but studies support its effectiveness, and it passes a most important test, the common sense test: each component has been shown to be beneficial for people with BD, and the different components work in complementary ways on different aspects of the illness.

Family and Couples Therapy

Your relationship with your partner, and your family's ongoing comfort and stability, should be a vital concern. In this regard, couples therapy or family therapy can be of great help. Bipolar disorder almost always has consequences for both members of a couple in which one has BD—in fact, it affects all members of a family. Seeking professional help with the problems that arise because of illness-related symptoms and behaviors is wise and usually successful.

Couples and family therapy use many of the same techniques as interpersonal therapy, but by definition they involve one or two therapists and the couple or family, all in the same room and all working on the same issues. It's not surprising how often thoughtful reevaluation and a positive change in destructive habits in thinking and behavior can improve things. This opportunity for professional help with a relationship can take a great burden off the individual partners, and couples and family therapy are often recommended as part of the treatment of BD.

CHOOSING A QUALIFIED (NONPSYCHIATRIST) MENTAL HEALTH PROFESSIONAL

As should be clear by now, along with your partner's psychiatrist, a psychotherapist may also become an important person in both your lives. You'll rely on this person to help you maintain emotional equilibrium, and maybe even your marriage or relationship. Choose wisely.

The need for and role of additional therapists are things the psychiatrist, patient, and partner should all discuss. For most of the work described in the previous sections, including cognitive-behavioral therapy, the therapist should have a PhD in clinical psychology as well as a license to practice in that field. Some licensed clinical social workers also have specialized training in CBT and are excellent therapists. Couples and family therapists are most often licensed clinical social workers; others are clinical psychologists with special training and experience in work with couples and families. The best way to locate this person will probably be through your psychiatrist, as this will be someone with whom not only you but also your psychiatrist will work. Everybody should be comfortable sharing information, except in rare instances in which something must be held secret.

The Academy of Cognitive Therapy has a national database of qualified clinicians. Local branches of the American Psychological Association and professional social work associations will also have lists of qualified and recommended practitioners. Hospitals and clinics will have staff and lists of providers.

When interviewing prospective therapists, the questions you should ask will be similar to those you would ask a psychiatrist:

- "What is your professional orientation?" Most will probably specialize in cognitive-behavioral therapy or related therapies, but they may also use a combination of approaches. Psychoanalysis has little or no role here; therapies heavily based on it, so-called psychodynamic therapies, have no proven efficacy in BD.

- "Are you state licensed?" Again, the only acceptable answer is "Yes."
- "About how long would you expect treatment to take?" Most therapists will not be able to answer this question without first evaluating the patient. This kind of therapy is usually relatively short term and focused, but it can be recurring as new problems arise or as support and problem solving are needed.
- "How much clinical experience do you have treating patients who have bipolar disorder?" Usually, the more experience, the greater the likelihood of success.

OCCUPATIONAL AND REHABILITATION THERAPIES

Sometimes psychiatrists refer bipolar patients for rehabilitation or occupational therapy. One form of "rehab" with which everyone is familiar is a treatment setting for alcohol and substance abuse. As we have seen, bipolar individuals frequently attempt to self-medicate with alcohol or drugs, and may become addicted. Rehabilitation therapy for substance abuse, often done in a day care or residential setting, may therefore be part of your partner's treatment. These programs help patients avoid exposure to unwanted drugs while they learn to manage cravings and gain coping techniques.

Bipolar disorder can lead to problems on the job and in other social interactions and responsibilities. For these problems, too, as for substance abuse problems, people with BD may spend time in specialized programs to learn or recover needed skills. Occupational and rehabilitation therapies for bipolar patients work with hands-on activities in practical, daily life settings such as work situations or community interactions—shopping, making appointments, and so on. By sharpening the skills needed to negotiate daily life (goal setting and task-oriented activities like managing medication and time), increasing self-awareness, and reinforcing the ability to succeed, these therapies can fight against residual symptoms of illness, such as depression, anxiety, or disorganized thinking. By giving the person structure and organized activities, they can help ameliorate symptoms of mania as well, and help keep a patient on the kind of regular treatment and daily schedule that can reduce the risk of new episodes of illness.

The ultimate goal of occupational and rehabilitative therapies is not only to help people with BD be successful in the workplace, although this is one goal. More broadly, they can help patients integrate the intellectual discoveries they are making in talk therapy into the day-to-day activities of living in the world.

Many hospitals, mental health clinics, and individual therapists offer rehabilitative and occupational therapies. In most big cities, there are patient-run clubhouses as well, or other community programs that can provide a variety of social interactions for skill building and the opportunity to learn new work skills, sometimes in jobs structured for people with BD or other psychiatric disorders.

As with the other therapies discussed in this chapter, your partner's psychiatrist should be able to help you get started with a referral to a qualified occupational or rehabilitation program or therapist with experience in working with bipolar individuals.

OTHER MEDICAL TREATMENT OPTIONS

Psychosocial therapies, like the ones described in the previous sections, can be immensely helpful—but they are not likely to be effective enough, used alone. If medication—the first choice for most patients—is not an option to be used in tandem with these therapies, certain treatments that work directly on the brain—the site of bipolar disorder—may also be effective.

Electroconvulsive Therapy (ECT)

Electroconvulsive therapy (ECT) has proven particularly useful for treating acute bipolar mood episodes. In a much cruder form many years ago, electroconvulsive therapy was known as "shock treatment" or "shock therapy." It gained a bad reputation, which in some measure it deserved. Over the decades, however, it has evolved. Modern electroconvulsive therapy is done under anesthesia. It does not produce horrifying muscle jolts, crackling noises, or pain. In fact, today it is considered one of the safer and more effective treatments for bipolar disorder (and also for unipolar depression).

Kitty Dukakis, wife of former Massachusetts governor and presidential candidate Michael Dukakis, cowrote a book about her success using ECT against intractable depression, informing the public about this often overlooked but successful treatment. Indeed, ECT is enjoying something of a resurgence in popularity today and is most commonly used in academic centers and high-end treatment settings.

Although ECT is often used only when medication has failed (possibly because most psychiatrists incline toward prescribing), it can be a good choice, especially for those who don't tolerate or respond well to medicines, or for severely depressed patients who can't safely wait for medications to take effect.

One upside is that ECT is a short-term therapy. It usually requires two or three sessions a week for two to four weeks. Although it is generally safe, the anesthesia needed to perform ECT can pose a danger to patients who have major health problems, such as advanced heart or lung disease. It frequently causes some degree of memory loss for events occurring during the period of treatment; but it rarely, if ever, appears to cause a general loss or decline in memory.

Patients sometimes feel groggy on waking, and they may also have confusion or head or jaw pain. In cases of short-term confusion, treatment is sometimes discontinued, or sessions are administered less frequently.

Once treatment is completed, depression may not return for months or years; sometimes treatments are continued on a less frequent, maintenance, basis, such as once monthly.

Although ECT is most often used to treat unipolar and bipolar depressions, it can also be used for mania. However, its efficacy against mania is not as well studied.

Transcranial Magnetic Stimulation (rTMS)

Transcranial magnetic stimulation, known as rTMS—the *r* stands for "repetitive"—may offer hope against bipolar depression, as well as other mental disorders. The procedure involves an electromagnet placed on the scalp, and the production of pulsed (repeated) electromagnetic fields. It does not require anesthesia and is usually done on an outpatient basis.

Generally, rTMS appears safe. Side effects often include mild headache, tingling, lightheadedness, or discomfort from muscle spasms from the electromagnetic pulse or from noise generated by the procedure itself. This possibility can be reduced through the use of earplugs during the process. Pain caused by contraction of the scalp or jaw muscles can be minimized with an over-the-counter pain reliever beforehand. There can, however, be more serious side effects, though these are exceedingly rare. They include seizures, hearing difficulty, and mania.

Although rTMS may hold promise, particularly for patients for whom medication is not a good option, we have to caution against undue optimism: as of this writing, the Food and Drug Administration (FDA) has "cleared," but not "approved," the treatment for use. This means that the FDA considers rTMS to carry no more than a moderate risk, but did not determine that it had been proven effective for any disorder. As yet, there has been no widespread use of rTMS; that is, so far, it has little in the way of a track record.

Neurofeedback

Biofeedback, in which information on such measurable bodily functions as pulse or blood pressure is revealed to a patient as a tone or other signal, has long been used in the treatment of some physical disorders, including hypertension and chronic pain. Through biofeedback, patients can learn to reduce their blood pressure or modulate distress. Neurofeedback is a form of biofeedback that targets brain function; the patient receives information (for example, on a video screen) about changes in brain waves or brain activity while painlessly hooked up to a monitor. It might help patients learn to ease anxiety or take the edge off depression, and could be useful as a supplemental therapy or when medication or other procedures are not workable.

Some practitioners say it can be used successfully against bipolar disorder itself. As of this writing, however, we know of no data to back that up.

By now, it should be clear that there are a number of effective treatments for bipolar disorder. Nevertheless, there is currently no cure. BD is something that you and your partner will live with over the long term. Along with maintaining consistency in taking medication and receiving psychosocial therapies, you will need to deal with a wide variety of life and relationship issues. In the next chapter, in Part Two, we'll look at an issue that is vital to people with BD and their partners: creating a support team of family and friends.

Part 2

Living with
Your
Partner

CHAPTER 6

Building a Support Team

I'm resigned to living with bipolar disorder for the rest of my life. The fear and shame are gone; I speak about my illness openly with both family and friends and have even ventured out into the public arena, sharing my story of my battle with bipolar disorder in Electroboy: A Memoir of Mania. *This was probably the hardest thing I had to do with my illness—to go public. But I did it because I . . . thought that my sharing my story . . . would bring people out of the closet to seek treatment, help family members in understanding their loved ones, and also help mental healthcare professionals in treating their patients.*

—Andy Behrman, author, *Electroboy: A Memoir of Mania*

At work, your partner is distracted but makes up for it by working around the clock to finish a project. After work, he is the life of the party, maybe gets a little too drunk. At home, the kids know to leave the room during his rages. Everyone accepts these personality quirks as part of the package. You're the only one who knows that your partner has been diagnosed as bipolar—and that can be a hard burden to carry.

You may both be afraid to stigmatize your partner as "crazy"—and risk stigmatizing yourself as well—by telling people about BD. Although you don't have to tell everyone, you do have to tell someone. If you are both going to live in the healthiest way possible, it is crucial to build a core support team of family, friends, and professionals who can help you. And that means you have to begin bringing to light what has probably, until now, been hidden or at least covered up.

Sooner or later, it will probably be impossible for your partner to conceal unusual behaviors from others. You may be asked about them—by concerned family members and close friends, coworkers and casual acquaintances. Eventually people will notice and want to know what's up.

Many people will simply make their own assumptions. Chances are, they'll blame circumstances or psychological factors—or you. Talk with your partner about how to handle any questions *before* the situation arises, so you can plan answers that will address the implied criticism of your spouse and help educate the questioner. Your therapists and support groups can help you think these issues through.

When Your Partner Asks You Not to Tell Anyone

If your partner has asked you to maintain secrecy, should you do it?

In most circumstances, certainly social ones, you should honor his request—at least for the moment. Everyone is entitled to privacy—it's not entirely unreasonable for your partner to expect you to help bear, in some degree of secrecy, the burden of a bipolar spouse. This is particularly true when the diagnosis is a new one.

Still, complete secrecy cannot—and should not—go on forever. Your best bet will be to talk with your partner when the symptoms are under control. Make it clear that you respect your partner's right to privacy, but that it is very difficult for you to maintain that nothing is wrong and to carry what is likely to be more than your fair share of the relationship with little outside emotional support from people who understand what is really going on.

You might also point out, if true, that others are not unaware that something is wrong, and it might help to explain the problem rather than leaving them to their opinions and speculations.

Together you can select an appropriate confidant—ideally, *more* than one.

WHOM SHOULD YOU TELL?

No question: sharing information about your partner's bipolar disorder with people who care can bring light and understanding to an area that has, until now, been dark and hidden. It can also significantly lighten your load, particularly if you choose your confidants wisely and can rely on them for support and assistance.

People who should know about your partner's BD usually include the following:

- All of your spouse's doctors, including the dentist
- Your children
- Your parents and your spouse's parents, if they are involved and engaged with both of you
- Other close family members or friends, at your discretion

People who may have to be told include the following:

- Your spouse's employer (though this is among the trickier things to accomplish), particularly if company medical insurance is involved in treatment
- Your own employer or coworkers, if things at home are spilling over significantly into your work life

LIVING WITH BD

Gloria

When my kids were young, I didn't know I was bipolar. I yelled at them a lot. And when I wasn't doing that, I was barely getting through the day. I know they didn't have it easy. They always looked at me like, what's she gonna do next? I remember thinking the same thing about my Pop.

It wasn't until they were in their teens that I finally accepted something was really wrong, and I got the diagnosis of bipolar. When I finally started to get stabilized, I knew I had to tell my kids. I realized I had been hiding an important part of myself from them. It felt like lying, and I didn't want to do that. I realized my Pop was probably bipolar too, and if I had known that growing up . . . I don't know, but I think things might have been different for me.

So I sat them down and told them everything about the moods, how they made me feel—everything. They were scared, but I could also see they were relieved. I remember my daughter said, "Well, that explains a lot!" She said it made her feel she wasn't to blame for a lot of stuff she'd been taking on herself—I didn't even know. My son said, "Does that mean I'll get it?" I told him the truth—I didn't know for sure. But if he ever thought it was happening to him, he'd have the tools to deal with getting help.

Telling them was hard, but I'm glad I got everything out in the open. It changed our relationship for the better. Now, with my grandkids, they know that Nana sometimes has moods; they get it. They do not take these things personally.

TELLING YOUR CHILDREN

How you speak to the children in your family, and what you choose to tell them, will depend on the ages of the children in question. Adult children may feel relieved to know that a parent's past behavior had a biological cause. And, of course, genetic information is important too, particularly for adult children who are themselves parents or would like to be.

Exercise particular care if you need to discuss your partner's illness with a younger child. Small children can't—and should not—be depended on to keep confidences. That kind of expectation places an unfair responsibility on the child. Also, requiring privacy suggests that the secret must be "bad."

When you're talking to small children, a matter-of-fact approach is best. They need reassurance—if you can truthfully give it—about their parents' well-being. They can be told, for example, that Mom or Dad isn't feeling well, but (if true, of course) is seeing a doctor and is likely to get better. It's very important for them to know that their own needs will be met when parents are going through a difficult time.

Adolescent children are likely to be concerned, and legitimately so, about whether they too have or will have the disorder. You can honestly tell them that the probability of BD is higher for them than for the average person, although everyone has some degree of risk. Make sure they know that if they do develop bipolar disorder, you know how to help them manage it. Doing what they can to stay healthy now—including avoiding alcohol and drugs and maintaining a good diet, regular exercise, and adequate and regular sleep—will instill good habits and moderate behaviors, which will also help later on.

Like younger children, adolescents may feel anxious about whether their needs will continue to be met. They might also express concern for their bipolar parent's well-being. They will need to know that they're not expected to become caregivers, although they might be called on from time to time to help out, as any family member might be expected to do in a crisis.

Your partner's doctor is likely to be willing and able to talk to your children. Of course, always let your partner know that you will be telling the children about the diagnosis and what it will mean for them, before embarking on any such discussion. It is best if the two of you can agree on what will be said and can talk to the children together.

General Advice for Talking with Children About BD

- Be honest, but tailor the explanation to the child's age. Older children can absorb a greater amount of information overall and more detail on individual issues.
- Take your cue from the child. Give as much—or as little—information as your child seems to want. Try to be clear and specific, and correct yourself if you explain something poorly or learn new information. Check back with the child periodically to confirm understanding. It can be helpful to ask children to tell you in their own words what they have heard, to make sure their understanding is accurate.
- Leave the door open. Let your child know he or she is welcome to talk with you again about any concerns, or to ask questions at any time. Set up a time to talk further.
- Make sure to listen to your child's concerns at least as much as you talk. Ask explicit questions, such as, "What do you think about what I've just told you?" and "Is there anything else you'd like to know?"

TELLING PARENTS

A big part of people's fear about telling family members comes from not knowing what reaction to expect. As a general rule, people will behave as they usually do. If your partner enjoys a good relationship with parents or siblings, chances are their reaction will be supportive. If they normally handle these kinds of things poorly, you and your partner might want to rethink whether telling them is a good idea. If you do decide to tell them, plan very carefully what you will share and how you will share it.

Parents generally dread the idea of their grown children calling into question their past parenting. You need to be careful that the conversation, should you decide to have it, not go in a direction that will make them feel blamed. Do this by sticking to the facts, avoiding any mention of past conflict, and using matter-of-fact language and tone. For example, "Jerry has been diagnosed with bipolar disorder. His doctor has assured us that this is a brain disorder—a medical condition. It doesn't have anything to do with the way he was raised, and it's nobody's fault."

Because of hereditary factors, siblings may also have BD or related disorders, diagnosed or not. Holding a discussion might prove helpful to them for their own sakes. In addition, if your significant other feels that apologies are deserved for past behaviors due to illness, a conversation would provide a natural opportunity to offer them.

You should consider telling your parents—your partner's in-laws—too, especially if they are very involved in your lives. It may be a little easier, because they won't feel responsible for the illness. If their relationship with your partner is not good, however, this could bring to the front old feelings and criticisms of you and your partner. Address such issues as openly and honestly as possible. Eventually, your parents may even feel more comfortable with your partner once they realize that some past problems were caused by a treatable illness.

TELLING OTHER FAMILY MEMBERS

How many other family members you want to apprise of your partner's bipolar status will depend on how involved these relatives are in your life, whether they have noticed problems, and whether telling them is more likely to lead to understanding or misunderstanding.

Most people share information on illnesses only with those to whom they are especially close, who might be able to help in times of need, and who they know will respect their privacy. Each case must be separately discussed and evaluated concerning the benefits and risks of sharing.

TELLING FRIENDS

Friends are among the few people whom we choose to have in our lives, and whom we can stop seeing if we find they are no longer rewarding or healthy to be around. Ideally, good friends support us through difficult times and depend on us to do the same for them.

Decide together which friends to tell, and how. You might start with friends you share, so that you can tell them together. It can be a formal invitation ("We have something we'd like to discuss") or a matter you let "casually" slip ("Bob's having a difficult time with his bipolar meds—oh, you didn't know?"), according to your style and the nature of your relationships. But even if you start casually, be ready to explain in detail, and decide ahead of time how much you wish to share.

Although you can't know beforehand exactly how your friends will react, you can expect a standard range of responses. Your friends will most likely want more information. ("I've heard of that—isn't that what Brittney Spears has? But I really don't know too much about it.") If you can provide information about BD generally, not just about your spouse, do so. If you know of books, Web sites, or other sources to steer them toward, by all means do that. We've listed a few in the Resources section at the end of this book. Interest is good!

Good friends will usually ask how they can help. ("Wow, I really appreciate your telling me about that. Listen, if there's anything I can do, just let me know.") Will one or both of you need someone to talk to sometimes? Take them up on this offer. Will you need someone to help out with child care in case of hospitalization? How wonderful to have someone you know you can call.

Often they will have noticed that there was a problem and will be relieved to finally know what it is and that it can be handled ("I wondered what was going on with you guys . . ."). Let them know you'll be happy to answer any questions you can. They will probably figure out for themselves that your partner is still the same person they've always known, but it can help to reinforce the truth that bipolar disorder is an illness a person *has*; it is not the person.

Other friends might want to share their own stories about BD, or those of their family members or acquaintances ("Hey, my Aunt Sara has that!"). Still others might react with unnecessary pity ("Oh dear! I'm so, so sorry!"). If this happens, it is probably meant kindly. Thank the person for her concern, and let her know that you and your partner are dealing with it successfully (if this is true), as people do with many illnesses. Who gets through life without health problems of some kind?

Of course, no matter how understanding their reaction, your friends will need time to process what you've told them. The information may come as something of a surprise or even shock. And it's possible that some friend will be sorry to have been told, but you probably won't encounter that situation often, if at all.

TELLING NEIGHBORS

Your neighbors, except for those who are also close friends, probably do not need to know the intimate details of your lives. However, you might need or want to tell your neighbors if

- You'll need emergency child care during a partner's hospitalization.
- Your partner has been acting strangely or badly in their presence.
- You're especially friendly with them and share local responsibilities, such as carpooling.
- They seem to have experience with bipolar family members and you can give each other mutual support.

TELLING EMPLOYERS

You will not necessarily need to tell your partner's employer about the diagnosis. Health coverage through work may be involved in paying for medication and treatment, but health care itself is a personal matter, with privacy protected by law. Exceptions, which are not uncommon, can arise at a small company where everyone works closely together, when your partner and her boss work closely together or are friends, or when illness seriously compromises your partner's job performance.

Your partner cannot be fired for being ill, but she can be fired for being repeatedly absent, ineffective, error prone, or unproductive, and illness can cause all these problems. Get advice from your partner's doctor about how best to talk to employers or to the human resource representative at work. Don't be afraid to share appropriate information when necessary. Often, changes in workload or schedule can be arranged to accommodate illness, especially if treatment is under way and symptoms can be expected to improve. Any large company has many employees with bipolar and other illnesses, and it is used to dealing with issues around illness.

Nonetheless, it is probably wise, as a general rule, not to share with your partner's employer or coworkers more than you must in order to make arrangements for her to do her job. Chapter Seven deals with workplace issues in more detail.

GROUPS

Attending a group—whether it is formal group therapy, led by a qualified therapist, or a less formal support group for bipolar patients, for their partners, or for both of you together—is an excellent idea. Good help, and plenty of it, can offer you and your partner your best hope for managing bipolar illness and its consequences, and for helping your relationship survive and grow.

Group Therapy

Group therapy is psychotherapy with a group of people all in the room at once, led by professional therapists. The therapists are often licensed psychologists or social workers; and as with individual therapy, your doctor, hospital, or local professional organization can help you find a group. The therapist is performing a professional service, so group therapy generally involves a financial cost. Group therapies have proved effective for psychiatric disorders, and most major insurance policies will cover at least some of the cost, if the therapy is prescribed by a doctor. Group therapies are as diverse as individual therapies. Most are based on the same psychological principles as individual therapies. But groups, which by their nature include multiple people, add more elements from research on social interactions. This makes them especially valuable for helping people see other viewpoints and monitor and test ways of interacting with others.

Some groups are more psychological in their orientation and content. Some are more social. Some are predominantly educational, teaching people about bipolar and other disorders, while offering the opportunity to share relevant experiences. Each type of group can be helpful, and one type does not necessarily replace the other. Patients and partners can sample one or more approach.

Before choosing a group, consider the advantages of each type of group for you and your partner. The two of you should discuss this together and with your partner's doctor and your doctor, if you have one. Ask the group therapist to describe the nature of the group and what will be expected of you and your partner. As always, if you start with a group but find, after a fair trial, that it doesn't meet your needs, find another group.

Support Groups

Support groups should not be confused with group therapy. Support groups are made up of people who come together regularly to share information and insights and commiserate with one another over a common problem. In contrast to group therapy, support groups usually do not charge, or will request small "dues" for things like room rental or juice and cookies. They are generally self-led—that is, directed by group members themselves—although some use professional or voluntary facilitators. Support groups are good places to share practical advice and help one another.

Face-to-face groups offer familiarity and, usually, consistency. Depending on the way the group is run, you might expect to see the same participants regularly, and helpful friendships often form.

Groups can provide emotional strength, coping tips, information about experiences with medication and other treatments, and validation of your own feelings and experiences. Bipolar support groups educate their members about medication and other treatments, expert clinicians and sites for care, and any developments in the realm of managing bipolar disorder. Plus—and this should not be underestimated—they can offer a place to complain freely and without judgment!

Of course, when considering any support group, common sense applies: good groups are supportive and helpful. They listen, comfort, share, help find solutions, and criticize respectfully. Bad groups scapegoat, demean, stigmatize, and make people feel worse. If you or your partner is not feeling better or getting the help such a group should provide, find a new group.

Finding a Bipolar Support Group

A good way to find a local support group for bipolar patients, their partners, or both is to inquire of your spouse's psychiatrist or therapist. You might also ask a trusted friend to keep an eye out. Search Web sites such as NAMI.org (the National Alliance on Mental Illness), DBSAlliance.org (the Depression and Bipolar Support Alliance), and others that deal in mental health.

NAMI lists a lot of information on its Web site, including how to find support. DBSA can help you find a support group, or form one if none yet exists in your area. Click on "find support" for a searchable map and listing of groups by state and zip code. Other sections of the site, http://www.DBSAlliance.org/Family Center and http://www.DBSAlliance.org/fc_events, contain resources for family.

You can type your geographical area, plus keywords such as "bipolar," "spouse," "partner," and "support," into your favorite search engine.

If no group exists in your area, or if, for whatever reason, you're not happy with the available choices, you might consider forming your own support group. If you can find at least one other interested party, you can, of course, work together.

Decide whether you would like your group to be self-directed or led by a professional therapist or facilitator. Finding a facilitator might not be easy, but it can be done. Although your own doctors are a good source for help in finding a facilitator, the facilitator should not be one of your doctors. You need to keep that relationship private. Your group will almost surely have to charge a fee to pay the facilitator if you choose a professional therapist for that role.

You can advertise your group by having cards printed or simply tacking up notices in likely places, once you have permission to do so. Ask your partner's psychiatrist whether you might leave some in his office, for instance, or whether he will at least recommend your nascent group to those who might also benefit from it. You can also post a message about your group online.

 ## LIVING WITH BD

Paul and Lisa

I'm crazy about my wife, always have been. But when she gets manic, she's hypersexual. My buddies think this is great, but it's not. I'm in the National Guard, so I'm sometimes away for weeks at a time. And if her meds need adjusting, or she "forgets" to take them and I'm not there to watch her, she's bouncing between moods. I can't trust her. At all. When she's stabilized, she's really apologetic for her behavior—begging me in tears to forgive her. I know she wants to be faithful, and knowing that helps a little, but it's hard.

A few months ago, I was so fed up I was ready to leave my marriage—most of my friends couldn't figure out why I hadn't left years ago. I called her doctor, begging him to do something, and he suggested we try a support group for bipolar patients and their spouses. Believe me, this is not something I would ordinarily do, but my wife jumped on the idea and I was desperate. I really do love my wife.

The people in the group were great. They all had stories like ours—some a whole lot worse, it was amazing—and they all poured out sympathy. It was like being with a bunch of war veterans—we bonded pretty quickly over our bad experiences, and I got a lot of really good advice. It also helped to see other people struggling to keep their marriages together, and succeeding.

Online Support Groups

In the absence of, or perhaps in addition to, a local support group, you might find a convenient community online. "Convenient" because you can participate when you have the time and inclination. You may take part as much or as little as you wish.

Online support groups offer much in the way of simplicity and comfort: you can log on when you want to, whatever time of day or day of the week. You wear what you like, disregard threatening weather, and receive responses or read other stories and questions from anywhere in the world.

There are several options *within* online groups. *Chat rooms* offer the opportunity for conversation (via messaging) in real time. *Listservs* are e-mailed messages that arrive in your inbox. Unless other arrangements are made, all e-mails go to all participants. *Message boards* allow users to post items and respond to others at their convenience. Most sites seem to use message boards or chat rooms.

One popular listserv, BPSO.org (for "Bipolar Significant Others"), often has a short wait time. If you join, you'll be asked to provide such information as your full name and address. If you sign up for this group, you might want to filter the messages into an e-mail box specifically for it. Otherwise, your inbox could fill very quickly!

Other sites, such as About.com, offer information about bipolar disorder, plus community forums in which anyone can participate. We have listed other excellent resources for the bipolar community in the Resources section at the end of this book.

Remember that anything put on the Internet might not remain private. Be careful about identifying yourself or sharing information that could harm you or your partner if it became public.

Handling Your Partner's Objections to Joining a Support Group

Your significant other might agree to go to a group with you, but object to your participating in a partner support group— that is, a support group that includes only those living with someone with BD, not the partner who has it. The most common reason for this objection is that spouses can feel threatened when they believe others are talking about them— as, in fact, you will be. Others might continue to deny that they have bipolar disorder, and a few might feel as if they must be pretty bad people if you need a support group just to deal with them.

Respond to such objections compassionately but firmly. Explain that bipolar disorder can be difficult for all concerned, and that information, empathy, and new coping skills can only benefit the both of you. Remind your partner that everyone there will be in the selfsame situation.

Joining an Advocacy Group

Joining a group that advocates for better treatment of people with BD, or for more research on BD, is a positive step you and your partner can take, either separately or together. This is different from joining a support group focusing on personal problems and needs, and helps bring you out of yourself and into the wider world.

The Depression and Bipolar Support Alliance (DBSA) and the National Alliance on Mental Illness (NAMI) are good places to start. Both groups advocate, hold informational lectures, and visit lawmakers. They also sponsor walks (like the many AIDS walks and breast cancer walks) to create awareness, show strength, and press politicians for parity coverage and monies for treatment and research. The core membership of DBSA is patients; the core membership of NAMI includes both patients and their relatives.

NARSAD, the world's leading charity dedicated to mental health research, was formed by NAMI, the National Mental Health Association, and the National Depressive and Manic Depressive Association. It funds research and also holds local events. Like the other groups, it can keep you informed about advances and opportunities, and give you contact with others in situations like yours and with those who can make a difference in policies.

Simply joining these groups can be empowering: you need no longer feel hopeless about what is or isn't being done to help you and your partner; you are actually out there helping bring about change.

Once you and your partner have come to terms with the diagnosis of bipolar disorder and have begun sharing information with selected relatives or friends about your circumstances, you may find that your life begins to move from covering up problems at home and dealing with confusion and secrecy, to learning to cope with the disorder in a healthier way every day. In the next chapter, we'll discuss bipolar disorder and the workplace, including how and when to tell the boss, and a variety of other issues.

CHAPTER 7

Bipolar Disorders and the Workplace

All I knew was that something was wrong, terribly wrong, and had been for about a year. . . . The message slips kept piling up and up until stacks of little white papers littered my desk. And yet, I somehow managed to keep my job. Unhappiness in a lawyer seemed to be the norm.
—Terri Cheney, Manic: A Memoir

For a person dealing with bipolar illness, the workplace can be a very difficult environment, where even mundane tasks or expectations can sometimes prove overwhelming. Preoccupied or unsympathetic employers or coworkers can unwittingly compound problems. Job loss has been known on occasion to send bipolar patients "over the edge," in some cases precipitating time in the hospital or suicide attempts.

TO TELL OR NOT TO TELL

A few strategies and pieces of information can help you help your significant other where job issues are concerned.

Reasons to Tell

There are many reasons your partner might need to consider telling an employer about his or her bipolar disorder. The following are some examples:

- He is taking a new medication and may need time for adjustment, or might demonstrate unusual behavior, such as grogginess, for a time.
- Her schedule doesn't allow for regular, restful sleep—which is an important factor in controlling the disorder.
- He's in the hospital as a direct result of BD.
- The disorder is affecting her behavior or performance on the job.

Keeping secrets is stressful, and a diagnosis of bipolar disorder is a very big secret to keep. Disclosure could help your partner's employers make sense of confusing behavior and unexplained actions, and could actually help your partner keep his job. The Americans with Disabilities Act (the ADA, discussed later in this chapter), makes it illegal to fire people just because they have bipolar disorder.

Reasons Not to Tell

The ADA doesn't solve every job-related issue, however; and disclosing the condition to your partner's personnel department, boss, and coworkers will probably not be an easy task emotionally and may put your partner at risk. A disclosure of bipolar disorder will inevitably color your partner's employer's and coworkers' perceptions of his job performance—"Did Jerry miss that meeting because the bus was late, or because he was off his meds?" Potential problems include discrimination, stigmatization, fear, and actual job loss.

Use this pro and con chart to help you put the decision into perspective:

Pro	Con
There's nothing disgraceful about the condition, any more than there would be about cancer or heart disease.	Prejudice and stigma about psychiatric disorders are still common in our society.
Carrying a secret is an enormous burden. Sharing lightens it.	You can't "untell" a secret.
The more people who know and are looking out for your partner, the more likely he'll be to get help before problems turn serious.	Word could get out and hurt your partner's chances for promotion or lead to job loss.
Sharing the information lessens the burden on the non-BD partner.	The employer is under no obligation to keep your partner's condition secret.
Lots of people have psychiatric issues, including bipolar disorder; maybe your partner's boss or family member does too.	Discrimination is illegal, but difficult to prove.
Talking about your partner's diagnosis is an opportunity to educate others and pave the way for future employees with BD or other disorders.	Your partner could be written off as "crazy."

Most people with BD struggle with the pros and cons of disclosure, but many do let their employer's know what's going on—if only for the health benefits and for specifically needed workplace accommodations. It's uncomfortable to feel exposed and scrutinized, but getting the "secret" out in the open may also open your partner to needed empathy and breathing room on the job. Ultimately, deciding whether or not to tell is a decision based on whether symptoms of illness are obvious anyway and need to be explained, and on whether—in your best assessment—the boss and coworkers can understand and help in a thoughtful way.

 ## LIVING WITH BD

Ron and Jan

My wife, Jan, was a second-grade teacher for five years before she was diagnosed. She's really good at her job—in fact, she was always given the kids who were considered hard to manage. She has a lot of energy—probably from hypomania, but I think she's just naturally something of a fireball—which the kids could really relate to. She's quite creative, too, and comes up with so many innovative ways to teach her kids. She received lots of praise from other teachers and from parents.

Then she got her diagnosis of bipolar 2. We both agreed that she should probably disclose it to her principal, for all the right and responsible reasons in addition to the health support and accommodation reasons.

Well, that was an eye-opener. Her principal seemed to take it well, but afterward she noticed that he was really keeping an eye on her. When she had to take time off, he questioned her—was she ill? Were her meds under control? Were the kids just too much for her to handle? And we think word might also have spread to the other teachers and some parents, even though the principal promised to keep it confidential.

So work isn't quite as pleasant as it used to be for Jan, but we both understand it's an adjustment for everybody. Everybody's trying their best.

When (and Whom) to Tell

Any of these reasons could make now a good time for disclosure:

- As a preemptive step, to head off potential problems
- To explain erratic behavior
- To explain absences

And especially if

- Your partner needs to request accommodation (a schedule change, telecommuting, or extra time off to adjust to new medication, for example)
- Your partner needs to submit benefit claims through the employer, rather than the insurance company
- The employer requires medical forms for extended absences, and your partner is anticipating such an absence

As for whom to tell, if your partner works for a midsize or large company, her human resources department is probably the best place to start. If you can, you or your partner should find out if initial inquiries and conversations are confidential. Schedule an appointment with the appropriate representative. Make a note of the person's name, direct line, and e-mail address so that you can get in touch again rather than have to tell the whole story to someone new the next time. It also won't hurt to send a note of thanks afterward, even if it's just a quick e-mail.

Company employee assistance programs (EAPs) can prove valuable resources. Find out whether your spouse's company has one—and whether *yours* does. EAP programs are usually confidential.

After the wheels are in motion, your spouse may have to talk to the boss.

TALKING TO THE BOSS

Talking to the boss can be a stressful endeavor for you and your partner, who will naturally worry about the effect of this disclosure on his job. Your partner's first move should be to discuss the pros, cons, and mechanics of disclosure with his doctors. You may also want to be in on this discussion, especially if it is necessary for you to be involved in the disclosure in some way. Any intervention must be handled carefully, as it may imply that your partner is not able to take care of his own responsibilities when that's not what you want to say. You must be able to establish that he usually can, but that, like many people, he is occasionally and temporarily indisposed by illness, and will recover soon.

Consider the Boss's Point of View

It can help to consider the discussion from the boss's point of view. A boss is a person, a person who may be decent and compassionate but who may also harbor prejudices or mis-conceptions. Most people are not well informed about mental illness, and your partner's boss may be in this majority.

The phrase "mental illness" can sound scary, especially to an employer, who is legally responsible for the safety of all workers. Serious episodes of workplace disruption are rare, almost never occur without clear warning signs, and almost never happen when the employee is receiving good treatment. But they make the news, especially if violence is involved, and such incidents as workplace shootings may pop into the forefront of the boss's thoughts. Fortunately, understanding of bipolar and other mental disorders is greater now than it has ever been, and this can go a long way toward countering fears.

Most likely, what the boss will want to know is, How will this affect things at work? Can the employee still do a good job? The boss may also wonder, "What are *my* responsibilities? Does this employee present a danger to me or to coworkers? Could *I* get into trouble if I don't handle this correctly?"

And just possibly, the boss will think something along these lines: "Really? My favorite cousin, Ed, was diagnosed bipolar 2. I'd hate for him to lose his job because of that. Or, I'm on Prozac for depression myself. I know what it's like to live with this sort of thing, and I really feel for you."

How to Tell and What to Say

Talking to the boss is stressful no matter what the topic of conversation. Your partner should make her disclosure when stable so that she can discuss these matters calmly and appropriately.

Once your partner has told the boss about her diagnosis, she should make certain the boss understands exactly what that means for job performance:

- Whether and how the condition is currently being managed (assure the boss that treatment is being carefully monitored, if this is true—and it should be true)
- What will probably remain *unaffected* (for instance, the quality of your partner's work; if it has been erratic because she was ill, this should be stated along with the fact that her skills remain intact and that with treatment she should be back to performing at her usual level)
- What kinds of accommodations, if any, will be helpful or needed (time off, different schedule, and so on)

Your partner should also invite the boss to ask any questions that need to be cleared up. Working together to find a solution puts employee and employer "on the same team" and fosters cooperation—at least ideally. This works best for an employee who has proven her worth to the company and can cite the fact that she has performed well. She can state with some confidence that she is likely to be back at full efficiency.

Some suggested language for framing the discussion:

"I like working here, and I want to do the best job I can. I have bipolar disorder; it's currently being managed by medication. However, I may need a dosage correction or other adjustment, which might require a few days off."

"I want to do a good job, and know I *can*. Would it be possible to [change my hours, allow me time off for medication adjustment, make up the hours, and so on]?"

DECIDING WHETHER TO TELL COWORKERS

Disclosing to coworkers is usually a matter of preference rather than necessity. It is common for coworkers to know when something is wrong, and being forthright can help, if your coworkers are caring people. Generally, we can get a feel for sympathetic, friendly "allies." Sometimes, however, we later find we've misjudged. And coworkers inevitably gossip. Once the secret's out, it is likely to spread around the office. In the end, your decision may just come down to whether it's more difficult to tell or to maintain secrecy.

Working and Medication

If there's any possibility that a new medication will cause drowsiness or motor coordination problems, your spouse should not drive, operate machinery, or perform other tasks requiring alertness until she is acclimated to the drug. Give her a ride to work, buy her a bus pass, encourage her to take a "personal day" on the first day she takes the medication.

A person adjusting to a prescription might appear to be ill, confused, or "out of it." It might be helpful for your partner to take time off or, if possible, to use vacation time to try new medications or dosages.

It may also be imperative that your partner make it clear to her employer (and coworkers, if appropriate) that looking ill or confused is a side effect of medication, not part of the illness.

HELPING YOUR BIPOLAR PARTNER APPLY FOR WORK

Even if your partner is well stabilized while she is applying for a new job, she can benefit from and may need your help when engaging in this process.

She might, for example, encounter thorny questions from prospective employers. People with BD frequently have spotty job histories—they may have been fired for not showing up (because they were too depressed to get out of bed), or they may have walked off the job impulsively while manic.

Such interview questions as "Why did you leave your last job?" and "How long were you employed by the company?" are common. Absences will usually have to be explained.

The key to getting any job is not defending one's past record but convincing the employer that the applicant is the best candidate. Mental illness, especially when it's well controlled, need not disqualify. Most employers look for problem-solving abilities, a strong work ethic, dependability, loyalty, and similar qualities. Evidence of past success and good references are especially helpful.

Be Prepared

You can help your spouse think about appropriate answers to interview questions. Employers do understand that people can become sick and then better. You are not required to document the nature of the illness or the specific diagnosis, if you wish to mention that you had been ill.

Counsel your partner to emphasize the qualities he can offer an employer. It might prove worthwhile to invest in a professional job coach or résumé service for your partner, for advice on presenting himself in the best way possible.

Other strategies include tenacity. The more interviews, the more applications, the more chances. Maintaining a regular schedule—such as e-mailing twenty resumes after breakfast, searching the job sites after lunch—can help your partner focus and increase his chances as well.

Preparedness gives your partner an advantage over other job seekers. The two of you can conduct practice interviews. Anticipating questions and gaining experience in "grace under pressure" can help put your partner more at ease and get him into "interviewing mode."

Advise your partner to research companies thoroughly and, if possible, learn the name of the interviewer or interviewers beforehand. Remind him that no job is worth getting overstressed about. He'll get the job or he won't. There will be other chances, maybe for even better jobs. The same is true for all of us, bipolar or not.

If your partner has a therapist, the therapist can be very helpful in dealing with issues of interviewing style, presentation of self, finding a job, or any job-related problems. Many of these problems are amenable to the very approaches to examining and modifying thought and behavior that are the professional strength of a good therapist.

Special Considerations and Attainable Alternatives

Even the best-sounding job can have drawbacks. Your partner should take into consideration the demands of any job she is thinking of taking or keeping.

Will there be long hours, travel, a frequently changing schedule? Remember that as a rule, caffeine, stress, lack of sleep, and irregular eating habits and hours are not ideal for a person who has bipolar disorder. If your partner is offered a "dream job" in which one or more of these will be a factor, perhaps together you can figure out a way to make the dream come true (telecommuting three days a week, job sharing, and so on).

Some careers—such as air traffic control, law enforcement, and the armed services—may be too stressful, or not legally possible. Perhaps it will turn out that for your partner, the job isn't a dream job after all. We all have to be realistic about what we can and can't handle. You and your partner should set aside time to talk about your partner's skills and wishes, but also about the dangers or limitations posed by illness:

- Lay out, ahead of time, what the attributes of a good job would be.
- List personal strengths and weaknesses.
- Catalogue advantages and disadvantages of current and possible employment.
- Be thorough and thoughtful about what responsibilities will and won't be manageable.

Thinking through these issues will prove to be enormously valuable over time. Choosing and staying with the right job will lead to more opportunities. Taking or trying to stay with the wrong job will lead to frustration, lack of success, and even episodes of illness. Help your partner be honest about what is possible and what won't work.

If a current job is too demanding, help your partner see the problem and look for alternatives. If full-time work does seem too stressful, help your partner consider part-time employment. Part-time or seasonal positions at busy establishments are often easier to find than full-time office work. Sometimes they even offer health and vacation benefits.

Also, in some cases a part-time or temporary job can become a stepping-stone. An employee who makes a positive impression enjoys a good chance of promotion or may establish the credentials and references needed for another job. Think of the clerk who advances to junior manager, then supervisor, then district manager—or who rises to middle management, from which he can look for other good positions within or outside the company.

Another option is volunteer work. It may not bring in needed money, but in the short run, such work can keep active someone who is partially disabled by symptoms, and help him (and you) gauge whether he is getting better and is ready for regular responsibilities. Volunteer work is also a way to demonstrate competence, get job references, and meet others who are regularly employed. Many institutions, including government agencies, self-help groups, and hospitals, can provide lists of volunteer opportunities.

Again, remember that you and your partner are not alone in assessing your options. Your partner's doctor and therapist can be very helpful in identifying an individual's skills and weaknesses and in determining good and bad job opportunities based on your partner's symptoms and course of illness.

When Your Own Job Is Affected

If you're working full- or part-time and dealing with a partner's active bipolar disorder, you will undoubtedly find that your work is affected too. This is another occasion when your company's HR department and its EAP, if it offers one, can be valuable.

If you enjoy a good relationship with your immediate supervisor, you might find it helpful to speak with her in confidence. Most people sympathize with the problems of others, provided they arise only occasionally. If your partner is in the hospital and you will need to adjust your hours, it may be wise for you to tell your employer. Under most circumstances, that's too much to handle on your own, and you don't want people to misunderstand why you must take some time off.

HOW THE AMERICANS WITH DISABILITIES ACT (ADA) AFFECTS PEOPLE WITH BIPOLAR DISORDER

Is bipolar disorder covered by the Americans with Disabilities Act (ADA)? No—and yes.

Many people assume that certain disabilities are automatically "covered" in the workplace by the ADA. In fact, no condition is *automatically* covered. Each case that comes before the Equal Employment Opportunity Commission (EEOC, the agency that enforces the employment provisions of the ADA) is considered on its own merits. That said, Congress recently broadened the definition of "disability" with the intention of covering a greater number of psychiatric conditions.

The ADA Amendments Act of 2008 should make it easier for persons with psychiatric conditions to show they have covered disabilities. For example, the revised ADA will permit an individual with bipolar disorder to receive coverage if she can demonstrate a "substantial limitation" in "major bodily functions," including neurological and brain performance. The ADA retains the three-part definition of disability (please see the next section), but makes clear that applying for and obtaining coverage should be much easier than it was before. That being said, this route is not necessarily easy, nor is success assured.

Understanding the Disability Application Process

When making decisions about whether a condition constitutes a handicap, the commission looks for specific evidence of a covered disability and for employer actions that unfairly treat a person who has a disability. There are three ways to show a disability under the ADA:

1. Having a physical or mental impairment that substantially limits a "major life activity," such as the ability to take care of oneself or the ability to concentrate
2. Having a record of having a substantially limiting impairment
3. Being regarded as having an impairment

Under the first two definitions, it is not enough to show a diagnosed psychiatric condition: an applicant must demonstrate that the condition substantially limits a major life activity or did so in the past.

Important: The revised ADA requires that positive effects of any "mitigating measure" be ignored in determining whether a person has a disability. This means that if the applicant uses medication to control the symptoms of bipolar disorder, the positive effects of the medication must be disregarded; the individual will thus be deemed to have a "disability" if she can show that she would be substantially limited in a major life activity without the medication.

Individuals who have bipolar disorder can meet the third definition by demonstrating that the employer made an employment decision such as hiring, promotion, taking disciplinary action, or firing based on an actual or perceived impairment. This means that if an employer takes an action based on the individual's bipolar disorder, that person may be covered under the ADA, and the employer may have to justify his action.

Being "regarded as having an impairment" does not mean that the employer's action was illegal, just that the employer must be prepared to explain himself to ensure that there was no discrimination.

The employer is expected to accommodate a disability if possible. However, even in the presence of a disabling condition, an employer can discipline or fire an employee for lack of performance.

Important Exceptions

It's unlawful to refuse to hire, or to fire, an otherwise qualified individual because of a disability. That said:

- The armed services are not covered by the ADA. Military law offers no protection for employment based on disability. However, *civilian* military personnel are covered by a sister law called the Rehabilitation Act of 1973, which is identical to the ADA and which also contains the expanded definition of "disability," effective January 1, 2009. The Rehabilitation Act prohibits disability discrimination by federal agencies.
- Small companies (those with fewer than fifteen employees) are not covered by the ADA, but may be covered under state antidiscrimination laws. Check your local, as well as federal, statutes.
- The ADA prohibits employers from asking about disabilities prior to making job offers. Your spouse should be advised not to disclose her bipolar status before receiving an offer or, ideally, proving she can do the job. At the same time, however, counsel her not to lie during the interview process if faced with an illegal question about disability. Although it's unlawful for employers to ask about disabilities during the interview, it's also a bad idea for the applicant to lie.

Doing so can backfire in a number of ways. Your partner can sometimes deflect an illegal question about illness or disability by responding that she has every reason to believe she can do the job and work effectively with others.

Some employers ignorantly—and illegally—ask applicants to fill out forms disclosing various medical conditions. An applicant's best course of action if presented with one of these may be to leave several, or all, questions blank. Employers don't always even look. If pressed, she can alert the interviewer that those might not be the kinds of questions the company should be asking and that medical information shouldn't be part of an interview. There are laws to keep this information private, to protect everyone. True, your partner might not get the job—but that ultimately could be for the best.

Requesting Reasonable Accommodation

The ADA states that, with certain exceptions, employers must make "reasonable accommodation" for applicants and employees with disabilities. That means allowing time off for doctor's appointments or hospitalizations, for instance. Other examples of reasonable accommodation might include schedule modifications to allow for medication adjustments, if the job's hours permit it. An applicant or employee should request a reasonable accommodation from an employer as soon as she or he knows that it will be needed.

However, companies are also protected. By the same rule, businesses are not obligated to spend so much money or effort on accommodation that it would cause what is known as "undue hardship." The definition of undue hardship, as with many legal matters, cannot be simply stated and varies with circumstance. If you and your partner feel your partner has experienced discrimination and you wish to take legal action, you will need to obtain expert, legal counsel.

Limitations of Protection

Keep in mind that the ADA will not protect all employees in all circumstances. Even if your partner's problems at work were caused directly by unchecked bipolar disorder, that doesn't guarantee that he can't or won't get fired. This is another reason for vigilance and prompt, sometimes preemptive, action. As always, your first line of defense is good treatment. Staying well and able to do a job is better than negotiating accommodations. However, if reasonable accommodations would help, your partner should not be afraid to ask for them.

If your spouse works for a small company or in a setting other than an office, check with the EEOC to see which rules and guidelines apply.

This can create a potential dilemma. Many people will feel reluctant to disclose their disorder—and not unreasonably so. Some employers will demonstrate enlightened, cooperative, innovative attitudes; others won't. There's still enough fear and misunderstanding surrounding mental illness that you can't be absolutely sure of any outcome. Together with your spouse, try to find the line between "oversharing" and disclosing what's necessary. Here again, your partner's doctor and therapist can be helpful. They have probably had other patients with similar experiences.

Important: An employee's request for reasonable accommodation—or disclosure of disability—is mostly confidential. (Under limited circumstances, information can be shared.) Further, any medical information about an employee should be kept in a separate file—not in a personnel file—and accessible only to very few.

For More Information

It may benefit you to become familiar with the ADA's requirements. Visit the Equal Employment Opportunity

Commission Web page at http://www.EEOC.gov/ for more information. Whether you and your partner consider bipolar disorder a disability or not, the protections of the ADA might someday prove helpful.

Another good resource is the Job Accommodation Network (JAN) information hotline (800-526-7234 or, in West Virginia, 800-526-4698). JAN is part of the U.S. Department of Labor and the President's Committee on Employment of People with Disabilities.

YOUR PARTNER MAY QUALIFY FOR SOCIAL SECURITY DISABILITY INSURANCE (SSDI)

Another kind of government benefit may apply to your partner with bipolar disorder, and that is Social Security Disability Insurance (SSDI). SSDI comes from Social Security trust funds—a fund your partner has already paid into by having worked. (Don't confuse it with SSI, Supplemental Security Income, which comes from general tax revenues and is a program instituted for lower-income persons.) SSDI was designed for those with limited ability to work, and it has the potential to make your lives more livable.

Does Your Partner Qualify for Disability Compensation?

In order to qualify for disability, your partner must have worked in jobs covered by Social Security and have a medical condition that meets the criteria for disability set forth by the Social Security Administration (SSA). There are several, so check with your local office or the SSA Web page (http://www.socialsecurity.gov/). Your spouse's treating psychiatrist should be able to refer you to resources for assessing eligibility.

The Five-Month Rule

As of this writing, there is a five-month waiting period before benefits commence. Therefore, it's advisable to apply as soon as possible after your spouse has become disabled.

You should also be able to answer the question, "When was your spouse last able to work?" The five-month rule was written in the 1950s, when it was assumed—rightly or wrongly—that virtually anyone could get by with the help of family or savings for five months. The regulation comes up for review periodically. The good news is that if your application is approved, you will receive a lump sum representing payment for the period beginning when you first applied.

Applying for Disability Benefits

Applying for SSDI can be a tedious process. Fortunately, the SSA offers help in completing the paperwork, and three ways to apply:

- Apply in person: Your partner can apply at the closest Social Security office. There are also instructions for third-party application, should that be necessary.
- Apply by phone: To do this, you will need to make an appointment. Call (800) 772-1213. If you're hearing impaired and using TTY, call (800) 325-0778.
- Apply online: Go to http://www.socialsecurity.gov/ and look for "disability."

What You'll Need

You can help your spouse by gathering medical records and rounding up such information as doctors' names, medications, dates of service, and last day of work. You will need the following when applying for disability:

- Your partner's Social Security number
- Names and numbers of your partner's doctors, social workers, clinics, hospitals, and so on, with dates of service
- Medical records, hospital ID numbers, health insurance information
- List of medications and dosages
- Work history summary
- Most recent W2 or tax form
- A birth certificate or other proof of age is advisable. The SSA will request the original, or a copy from the issuing body.

Children under age nineteen or still in high school may be eligible for auxiliary benefits. Later in the process, you may need to provide your marriage license and Social Security numbers and proof of age for each family member.

If you don't have all the documents you need, begin to fill out the forms anyway, or have your partner do so. The SSA should be able to help with missing info.

If benefits are approved, the SSA will review your spouse's case periodically to make sure they are still necessary. For more complete information, go to the SSA Web site or call (800) 772-1213.

Dealing with the outside world of jobs and friends is only half our lives. Once you and your partner have come to terms with the diagnosis of bipolar disorder, you may find that your life at home begins to move from covering up problems and dealing with confusion and secrecy to learning to cope with the disorder in a more healthy way every day. In the next chapter, we'll discuss the basics of effective communication and some strategies for coping with the issues of daily life.

CHAPTER 8

Communication and Coping Skills

Even when I was fighting with my husband, or so manic I seemed to be flying, there was a part of me that dispassionately observed what was going on and knew it was crazy. But I couldn't stop my actions. I said, "Self, you're nuts. You need to stop this," but I'd keep right on doing whatever crazy stuff I was doing. It takes more understanding than most people have to realize that the person cannot control his or her actions when they are manic or depressed. Not having control of your moods means not having control of your actions.

—Jane Thompson, *Sugar and Salt: My Life with Bipolar Disorder*

Although it's doubtful that your partner's symptoms would disappear if there were no stress in his or her life, certain situations—such as travel, lack of sleep, and conflict—seem to contribute to triggering bipolar symptoms. Thus it's important to avoid, minimize, or at least plan ahead for such situations. A relationship with less conflict will help your partner keep his moods stabilized and will help you relax, knowing that the likelihood of an episode of illness has been reduced.

Of course, no one can completely avoid stressful situations and unpleasant moods; they are just more potentially dangerous when bipolar disorder is a factor. Sharing feelings and observations can reduce the possibility that unaddressed disagreements and tensions will grow into major conflicts, and can help each member of a couple feel more comfortable in the relationship. Planning ahead can help avoid unnecessary stress and save each member of the couple from being faced with making important decisions urgently and without carefully considering the alternatives.

Many of us take life as it comes and avoid the difficult conversations. This approach is generally not conducive to healthy communication, and it's especially unwise with bipolar disorder. Finding the time and ways to talk about things, particularly difficult things, is crucial.

Not just any time is right. Knowing when you can and can't talk about problems is important. Adapt the advice in this chapter according to your partner's diagnosis and current symptoms. For example, if your bipolar 2 partner is angry, you may be safe trying to fend off a verbal attack through communication and coping skills. However, if your partner has bipolar 1 disorder, your reaction may need to be different. It is more likely that his anger may become rage, and rage could spiral into dangerous behavior, including physical violence. (See Chapter One for more about bipolar 1 and bipolar 2 diagnoses.)

Similarly, it is rarely possible to argue someone out of a delusion when that delusion is deeply believed during an episode of illness. You may, however, be able to discuss the delusion when your partner is well or at least less symptomatic, and she may learn to identify the delusion for what it is: a false belief.

Communication Basics

- DO listen attentively and with respect.
- DO couch any necessary criticism as positively as possible.
- DO praise your partner often (and honestly).
- DO avoid physically threatening gestures or behaviors, such as shaking your fist or invading your partner's space.
- DO stick to the topic at hand.
- DO say what's on your mind, but say it without blame or insult.
- DO keep your voice calm and modulated.
- DO give your partner the "last word."

- DON'T interrupt.
- DON'T make threats.
- DON'T bring up past or unrelated conflicts.
- DON'T blame or belittle.
- DON'T get involved in circular or no-win arguments. Know when to stop.

STRATEGIZE AND SET LIMITS AHEAD OF TIME

When your partner is already showing symptoms of a manic or depressive episode, it may be difficult to make yourself heard and understood. One technique that has proven helpful for many couples in which at least one member has bipolar disorder is to sit down together between episodes—when your partner is stabilized—and discuss symptoms and their possible triggers, as well as what steps each of you should take if symptoms reappear.

For example, your partner's symptoms might include such behaviors as pressured talking or paranoia. If you see evidence that your loved one is headed toward a manic episode, but she dismisses your concerns—not uncommon with BD—you can use your list to remind her that what she is experiencing (or what you are seeing) is a symptom and that there is an agreed-on plan of action that should be implemented. Often, this plan is just alerting your partner's doctor.

Strategize

Work on conflicts and plans for dealing with them each time the disorder is under control. During those calmer times, review your past experience and the success of your plans for dealing with symptoms. Ask your partner for suggestions about how to deal with typical disagreements.

In any kind of clash, but particularly where bipolar behaviors are concerned, prior planning can spare you from making decisions in an atmosphere of haste or threat and will help avoid unforeseen, uncontrolled, and unwanted consequences. Be clear with your partner about what kinds of behaviors will require you to call for help from doctors or even the police.

Set Limits

You should review acceptable and unacceptable behavior and discuss consequences—ideally, before conflict occurs. Let your partner know that behaviors such as verbal and physical abuse are inappropriate and dangerous, and that you will not tolerate them. You will probably both agree that they should not be tolerated. With these ground rules in place, you can more effectively, or at least more comfortably, walk away from an outburst, request a "time out," or call for help.

For example, Mika received a call from her bipolar boyfriend right in the middle of a class. For the hundredth time, he'd gotten into a panic about a work problem that in actuality was probably of little consequence. She apologized to her teacher and classmates and brought her cell phone out into the hall—where she made the mistake of trying to reason with the man. She pointed out that the situation he was worried about had come up many times before; that if things got so bad that he lost his job, they would cope; and that she was, after all, busy at the moment—as he well knew. The boyfriend did not calm down. His call only served to agitate them both. And Mika missed the rest of her class.

A firm, noncommittal approach might have worked a lot better. If they had agreed on limits beforehand, the conversation might have gone like this: "I know you're upset, but I'm in class now. I can't take another call until my class is over. I should be home by noon, and we'll talk about it then. I'll see you soon." Then she could end the call without feeling she had not addressed the issue at hand.

EFFECTIVE COMMUNICATION STRATEGIES

Communication between even the most calm and rational partners can be problematic. Misinterpretation is common. Add the perceptual, cognitive, and emotional difficulties of a psychiatric disorder, and misinterpretation is almost a given. Nonetheless, you might be surprised how often the basic rules of effective communication, consistently applied, can transform a no-win argument into meaningful discussion and eventual understanding and agreement.

Even couples who are not dealing with BD have problems communicating—and it's hard not to react in kind when you're being verbally attacked. If you've ever been short-tempered or mean to your partner, if you've ever said something like "Stop acting like a baby!" or had an interchange that led to statements like "I'm an idiot? *You're* the idiot!" you're certainly not alone—BD or no BD. Forgive yourself, forgive your partner, and then learn some effective ways to communicate.

At first, unfortunately, *you* will probably be the only one practicing effective communication skills. At least one of you needs to be in control; and because your partner is most likely to be out of control during the heat of the moment, you would be wise to step up and take charge of guiding the change in the style of the discussion. And you should start with the expect-ation that improvement will take patience and practice.

That means you can't use one technique, get frustrated when it doesn't work, and give up. Recognize that you are in this for the long term and that there will be a learning curve for each of you. But with repeated effort, and perhaps coaching and guidance from individual or couples therapy, you will both begin to make progress. An open-mindedness to take sugges-tions and try alternatives, and persistence in attempting to find the right approaches for you and your partner, will often lead to improved communication and a happier, more rewarding relationship.

In addition to the information in this chapter, aimed specifically at bipolar couples, many books have been written about interpersonal communication. In fact, communication techniques intended for parents and children may come in handy in other relationships, too. We list a number of com-munication books in the Resources at the back of this book.

The following techniques are generally helpful in commu-nicating and may be especially important when interactions are complicated by symptoms and episodes of bipolar disorder.

"I" Statements

"I" statements give you a way to frame your comments to reflect the way you feel, without placing blame. For example, it's quite common to blurt out in frustration, "You're always so negative!

Why can't you say anything nice to me?" But, as you know from experience, this kind of comment is more than likely to put the other person on the defensive. A better comment, and one that reflects where your anger is really coming from, is this: "I feel frustrated when you say things like that to me, and it makes me not want to be around you." Or you may snap, "Stop talking at me like that! Can't I get a minute to myself?" A better response would be, "I need some time alone right now." The former statement is heated and may be taken as insulting. The latter is calm and matter-of-fact.

It's not always easy to frame "I" statements in the middle of an argument, but with practice, you will get better at it. It's worth putting some effort into trying. Corny as "I" statements may sound, they really work to defuse anger. Instead of being challenging or accusatory, they are statements of your feelings and concerns and invite the other person to see things from your vantage point.

If What You're Doing Isn't Working . . . Try Something Else!

Although everyone's situation is different, this bit of solid advice really does apply to everyone: *If what you're doing isn't working, try something else.* Often the "something else" can be something quite simple. Solutions to problems frequently appear when people just take the time to consider doing things a different way.

For example, one bipolar man whose wife worked at home would return from his office each evening, head for the kitchen garbage pail and then get angry, escalating into a full-blown rage. His wife felt that she had enough household chores and that this one was his.

His wife grew to dread their evening routine: every night, her husband would come home, check the garbage, then curse

(continued)

(*continued*)

and complain because he felt there was too much of it—again. She wasn't prepared to take out the garbage herself, but she did find something quite simple to change: one day, she simply asked him to take the garbage out in the morning, when he generally felt more agreeable, instead of at night, after the stresses of the day. Problem solved.

Listen and Reflect Back

Listening to what your partner is saying and reflecting back what you heard in your own words show that you are paying attention to what your partner is saying and at least trying to understand. Listening and reflecting also allow your partner to clarify her point if you misunderstood her. Instead of engaging in an argument, ask your partner to tell you why she's angry. Then let her know what you heard.

Share Feelings and Understandings

Try letting your partner know that you truly understand what he's saying, and that you are taking it seriously. For example, "Oh, I think I understand something I didn't understand before—you're upset because you feel like I don't listen to you. Is that what you're saying?"

You can also make your partner feel better understood by acknowledging his feelings, adding something like, "I know that makes you feel really bad. I'm sorry if I hurt your feelings."

Talk to Solve Problems, Not to Win Arguments

Stick with this kind of communication and use all the tools we've discussed, if necessary. Don't let your discussion devolve back into the same old competitive argument you always have. You're not trying to win an individual victory; you're trying to achieve an improvement in your relationship.

Be the leader in helping your conversations evolve into opportunities to share experiences and feelings, and into discussions of mutually acceptable solutions to problems. Continue to bring the conversation back to what is being done and said in the here and now, and keep seeking to find and reinforce areas of understanding.

Offer Sympathy

If your partner is irritable, he is likely to be feeling very sensitive to every little nuance. This means he is more likely to take offense or misinterpret. Always bring yourself back to basics—don't react to the words; do attend to the underlying issue. He's feeling overly sensitive, he's uncomfortable, he needs and deserves sympathy. For example:

YOUR PARTNER: What? Why are you looking at me like that?
YOU: I just want to know what you might like for breakfast.
YOUR PARTNER: Nothing. I'm not hungry. Leave me alone.
YOU: I'm sorry you're not feeling too great, honey. Would you like to talk about it?
YOUR PARTNER: No.
YOU: All right. I'll check back with you later. In the meantime, please let me know if you change your mind.

Remember that bipolar disorder is sometimes quite variable from hour to hour, and even minute to minute. If this technique fails, you can make a note of how long the average episode or conflict lasts, and remind yourself that, in time, it will likely be over.

Communicating Through E-mail

In some cases, e-mail holds distinct advantages over spoken communication. Although it's true that it's harder to convey tone in e-mail than in spoken conversation, e-mail and other written interactions allow you to think about what you want to say and to stick to the issue at hand. If you're unused to communicating this way, give it a try, especially if you often find conversations devolving into arguments. E-mail can delay or buffer reaction to certain characteristics in a relationship that may be troublesome at the moment, such as tone of voice. Although e-mail can convey this tone, it allows the recipient to read it when ready and to respond when willing. It's an easy way to avoid an immediate, emotionally driven response.

SUPPORTIVE STRATEGIES

The underlying message of good communication with your bipolar partner is this: even if your partner frequently blames you, launches verbal attacks, refuses to speak, pouts, or makes life unpleasant in similar ways, *limit your reaction.* Your partner is probably not so much angry at you as not feeling well and not able to contain his feelings. What he says and does when he is not feeling well is more a reflection of his mood than of his underlying opinion of you or anyone else. Don't mistake the illness for the person.

Once you've done that, and you're no longer reacting to symptoms as if they were intentions, then what? Here are some good coping strategies you can employ to make further progress.

Use Positive Reinforcement

Positive reinforcement—rewarding good behavior, praising even small acts of kindness or any constructive act—is among the most valuable strategies of supportive interaction. Initially, it may feel strange to praise simple things that your partner should be doing naturally—taking medication regularly, helping with housework or child care, or earning a living—but do it anyway: compliments are rarely wasted. This is good advice in any relationship, and indispensable when living with someone diagnosed with BD.

Voice Your High Expectations

When people know our expectations are high, they tend to want to see that we're not disappointed, that we retain our positive image of them. When things get sticky, such statements as "I've always known you to be respectful" or "I'm sure you didn't mean that unkindly, but it felt unkind" can go a long way to helping your partner see the interpersonal consequences of things he might say or do, rather than remain unaware of or defensive about his statements or actions. Again—good advice in any relationship, and effective when dealing with BD. (Conversely, *never* express your reaction as disappointment—"I'm so disappointed in you; I expected more." This will only make your partner feel worse and share less than he or she already does.)

Turn Negatives into Positives

A related communication technique favored by experts—because it works—is to talk in terms of "positives," even when expressing unhappiness with your partner. This is similar to the strategy behind "I" statements, discussed earlier.

For example, replace the hurt accusation "You never touch me anymore" with a compliment: "I miss those wonderful backrubs." If you have doubts about how this works, imagine your partner saying positive things to you and reflect on your feelings.

Avoid No-Win Situations

No-win questions—including "Catch-22s" or "double-meaning statements"—are verbal dilemmas: choices between equally unappealing alternatives. Clearly, answering a question like "Are you a complete idiot?" with yes or no is a losing scenario for you. A better choice is to answer with a serious question: "Do you see me that way?" or "What's wrong? Can I help?" Your partner is speaking this way out of frustration; don't respond the same way. Your answer needs to help defuse the situation.

Avoid Inappropriate Anticipation

Inappropriate anticipation is another conversational trap. In this situation, one person hears a message that has not been spoken and responds to that. For example:

YOUR PARTNER: I think I'll have a wedge of that cheese I like.
YOU: Oh. Okay.
YOUR PARTNER: Something wrong with that?
YOU: No. Not at all.
YOUR PARTNER: Well, why are you acting like that?
YOU: Like what?
YOUR PARTNER: All weird. What's the matter with the cheese? Does it smell bad? Well, thanks a lot. Now I'll never eat that kind of cheese again!
   Or:
YOUR PARTNER: Are you still planning to put up those storm windows?
YOU: Yeah, I guess so. Why?
YOUR PARTNER: Well, you promised you would!
YOU: So . . . ?
YOUR PARTNER: Now, you're saying you won't. You're breaking your promise!

In both examples, the responder gives too vague an answer ("Oh. Okay" and "Yeah, I guess so"), and the initiator reads negative messages into it. This may not seem fair—and it might not be a problem if you were having a conversation with a nonbipolar friend. But in a relationship with a person diagnosed with BP, it can be a real issue. Remember, one of the symptoms of bipolar disorder is finding hidden meanings, often threatening ones, in normal events or interactions.

Definite replies can sometimes avert this conflict. If your response was clear and still misunderstood, or was unclear but received an excessive reaction, go over the conversation with your partner calmly: "Wait a minute. I think I might have given you a mistaken impression. Let's go over what we said to make sure I explained my position as well as I could have."

Act "As If"

You've probably heard the phrase "Fake it 'til you make it." Twelve-step programs also call this acting "as if." It's not a new idea. At the turn of the twentieth century, the American psychologist and philosopher William James was famous for this advice. He wrote, "If you want a quality, act as if you already had it. Try the 'as if' technique." The premise is simple but powerful: when you act the way you would like to behave—patient or concerned or grateful, for example—you are actually practicing that behavior. Over time, this can develop into your natural response.

For example: you're both expected at an event, and your partner, as so often happens, is terribly late. On top of that, he's lost his car keys—again. Your worst-case-scenario response is to say, "Again? I can't believe it! You always do this!"

To which he might respond, "You probably hid them somewhere, under your mess!"

The outcome? You never get to the party, and you're both furious.

Instead of expressing frustration, try this. Act as if you had all the patience in the world. Offer to help search, but if he wants to search alone, let him search for as long as he needs. Calmly sit down and watch television or read the paper. Tell him again that you're still willing to help but that you're also willing to wait. You'll be ready whenever he is. Yes, it reinforces the behavior you're trying to discourage; but it also expresses your compassion toward a person who truly can't control his disorganized behavior. Even better, by pretending to feel relaxed and magnanimous, chances are you really will begin to feel this way. And you are also modeling the same calm, accepting behavior you would like to encourage in your partner.

 ## LIVING WITH BD

Heather and Max

My husband, Max, can really hold it together around a lot of people, but in private, he'll just dump his mood on me. We'll be at a party and everything will be great, he'll be socializing, but as soon as we're out the door, he'll say something cutting. It was crazy making at first.

Finally, I figured out he felt free to do this because he felt safe around me. He knew I wasn't going to leave him because of it—I loved him. But I really didn't like it at all. I didn't like being someone he could feel free to dump on, and frankly I didn't think it was helping him—when he was calmer, he felt terrible about it, too.

We'd been talking about ending our marriage for a few years—it just seemed like we always spiraled down into the same old issues. But when I was able to respond to his criticisms in a healthier way—my therapist's words—it actually made me feel empowered. Even if I was just silent, and stopping myself from saying something horrible back, or running to the bedroom in tears, or slamming the door, I felt like I was in charge: I was doing something to change the nature of our interaction. And it did make a change—just modulating my response was such a shock to him that he began treating me with more respect.

One great trick to help me restrain myself is this one I learned in a support group. Every time he'd go off on a rant, that would be my signal to reward myself. I'd be quiet and just count. For example, I'd promise myself ten minutes of guilt-free Internet time wasting for every one of his muttered curse words, or a dollar spent on something I enjoyed for each cutting remark. You'd be surprised how fast those rewards could add up!

I know things will never be perfect, and that these episodes will happen from time to time, but I feel calmer about them now, more able to handle them and myself. And I think my being calmer is helping him be calmer, too. I'm looking forward to this next phase in both our lives.

COPING WITH MANIA

The best way to deal with virtually any treatable illness is to catch and address it early. Extra vigilance is needed in dealing with BD, because people experiencing the beginnings of mania typically feel good—which hardly makes them inclined to seek help. Two great indicators of impending mania are lack of sleep and speed talking or pressured speech. At the first sight of these symptoms, implement a plan of action, ideally one you and your partner have discussed ahead of time.

If your partner starts talking a mile a minute and won't tolerate any interruption, make an appointment—or at least schedule phone time—with her treating doctor. Together you may be able to head off a serious episode of illness or at least make plans to cope with the episode.

Take a Break

It can be exhausting living with a person who is bipolar, particularly if symptoms are common and when you feel that you are putting out a great deal of effort and not seeing immediate results. In this case, a short break from your partner might give you a much-needed change of perspective. If you have the time, take a walk outside. If you can, you may even want to arrange for a mini-vacation by yourself or with a friend for a day or more.

Even if you're able for only a few minutes to get away from a partner who's behaving badly, do it. Take a break: go into another room, listen to your favorite music, pet your dog, watch a favorite video clip.

React Calmly and Rationally, Even to Rants

Some people who have bipolar disorder tend to "go off," ranting at you or at others. This can be upsetting, no matter how many times you have experienced it, and your impulse may well be to yell right back. This won't lead anywhere good. There are better strategies you can employ.

The best way to deal with a partner who is ranting is to stay calm and rational yourself. Let your partner feel heard and understood, then see if you can work toward a desired outcome.

For example, if your partner calls you a controlling bitch because you ask if he's going to his psychiatrist appointment, resist the temptation to answer in kind. Take a deep breath, if needed, and say something along these lines: "I know you feel as if I'm nagging you, but it's important to me that you keep this appointment. We've had problems with you making, and then breaking, plans." You might add: "What would be a better way to remind you?"

Also remember: grumpiness can be tolerated, but if you feel unsafe, get yourself and your children away from your partner immediately. If the situation appears urgent, take her to a hospital right away or call for help. (See Chapter Eleven, "Dealing with Emergencies.")

 ## LIVING WITH BD

Mel and Elaine

Even though Elaine sees a psychiatrist regularly, takes Lamictal, and has had a reduction of symptoms, I wouldn't consider her "all better." Depending on the episode, she might have anywhere from six to ten of the symptoms listed for bipolar in the *DSM-IV* manual.

When she's "high," it's pretty unpleasant. One of the most frustrating things is, there's no rational discussion of the situation possible. She treats my suggestions and questions like attacks on her. Frustratingly, most of the anger and irritation she feels when "high" she does not recall when *not* high. When she's "low," she promises to be less nasty and hostile and more reasonable and less accusing—but when she's "high" she forgets all about this or dismisses those vows as having been made under pressure.

There's such a complete personality change that it's as though she is someone else entirely. Nearly all the characteristics that attracted me to her—her kindness, her sense of humor—are absent when she's high.

One thing that does work for us is to spend time away from each other during her manic phases. If I can be away all or a large part of a day, that can help me deal with her symptoms when we're together. And it's just the same if she goes away. We both have more patience for the times we need it.

COPING WITH DEPRESSION

Episodes of depression are more common than mania and can precede an episode of mania. They often begin with low mood or sadness; a decrease in interest, pleasure, and activity; and lowered confidence and drive. Even mild depression usually brings trouble with sleep, including feeling fatigued and sleeping too much, or trouble obtaining restful sleep. Any of these signs requires that your partner seek the counsel of his treating doctor. Addressed early, a long or deep bout of depression may be avoided.

For deep depression—your partner talks about suicide, stops eating, or can't seem to get out of bed—a consistent, loving pressure to get to a psychiatrist is essential. Stress the advantages for *your partner*—he could feel much better soon— rather than for you or other family members. However, if symptoms are serious and threatening to job or relationships, take action quickly. If symptoms are threatening to life, the situation is urgent: immediate action is critical. If necessary, take your partner to a hospital for treatment. (See Chapter Eleven for details on how to cope with this emergency.)

If your partner has already been in treatment for six months or more and still shows signs of obvious depression or mania, you could suggest that she bring up changing medications or dosages, ask for a consultation, or explore looking for a new provider. You might want to attend a session with her, in case the doctor, for whatever reason, isn't getting a clear picture of her situation.

Sometimes, perhaps because of memory problems or embarrassment, people who have bipolar disorder have difficulty reporting events accurately. In fact, studies show that most patients—not just people with BD—frequently minimize their symptoms when talking with their doctors. Some people do this because they are afraid of tests or treatments; others may be reluctant to offend the doctor by suggesting that treatment isn't working. Often they just don't want to be seen as ill.

If your partner is afraid of the consequences of starting or changing treatment, suggest that getting a consultation on alternative treatments does not necessarily mean he has to start them. Also keep in mind that people who are depressed often think negatively, and out of hopelessness may reject any help offered, and those who are manic may reject help because they do not feel they are ill. Don't yield your position if you see clear symptoms. Steady, respectful encouragement often leads to success. Abandoning the attempt to get treatment always ensures failure.

Basic Coping Skills

1. **Keep your sense of humor and encourage your partner to do the same:** This does not, of course, mean being indifferent to your partner's needs or suffering, or ignoring your own problems. It does mean paying attention for things that are ironic, absurd, or just plain funny about your situation, and enjoying as much of your experience and as many of your interactions as possible.

2. **Don't take things too personally:** We can only see the world as it relates to us, and we tend to interpret everything as being about us; but most things aren't. Your partner may be out of control, but you don't have to be. Learn to detach from your partner's behavior and to mentally separate your partner from his or her symptoms. When your bipolar loved one goes into a rant or becomes irrationally irritable, this behavior is a symptom—like coughing or running a fever. As long as you've done all you reasonably can to help manage the illness medically, it's important to keep some emotional distance when unpleasantness starts.

(continued)

(*continued*)

3. **Expand your world:** Look to your support team, your friends, positive family relationships, volunteer activities or paying work, creative pursuits, and whatever else you enjoy as a supplement to your primary relationship. Maintain friendships and interests outside your home. If you make your spouse your only friend, and your home life your only interest, you'll find yourself unnecessarily limited, frustrated, and without the means to relieve your frustrations.

4. **Get adequate rest, exercise, and nutrition:** This is good advice for anyone. Even if you can't ensure these for your partner, make sure to get them yourself. You will not only set a good example but also find it easier to cope if you're well rested, well nourished, and in generally good health.

5. **Set clear boundaries:** Bipolar is a serious disorder. You can't refuse to accept a partner's delusions or depression, but you *can* refuse to accept such behavioral symptoms as verbal sniping or physical abuse. Discuss and make clear which behaviors are acceptable and which are not.

6. **Cultivate patience:** If you don't always have patience with your partner, start by having patience with yourself. As you cultivate patience, it will grow. Living with another person is hard. Living with a person who has bipolar disorder is that much more so. You can expect some difficult times. Patience will make them easier to endure.

These are only basic guidelines for improving communication and interpersonal behavior in a relationship. Chronic marital problems generally respond well to professional therapy. If poor communication and bad interactions have become problems in your relationship, you'd be well advised to consider short-term couples therapy. In the next chapter, we'll explore techniques for dealing with life issues that can trigger negative or even dangerous behaviors.

CHAPTER 9

Coping with Negative and Dangerous Behaviors

*Seven years ago I had an attack of pathological enthusiasm. . . . I
believed I could stop cars and paralyze their forces by merely standing
in the middle of the highway with my arms outspread.*
—Robert Lowell, poet, and Pulitzer Prize winner

In December 2005, a man named Rigoberto Alpizar was
killed by federal marshals at Miami International Airport
after running off of an airplane in an agitated fashion, clutching a backpack to his chest. The marshals believed he was
carrying a bomb. It was later determined that he was not.

In 2003, twenty-seven-year-old Jayson Blair, on course to a
brilliant career in journalism, shocked friends, colleagues, and
the general public when it was learned that he had fabricated
dozens of news stories during his tenure at the *New York Times*.

Between 2006 and 2007, respected historian and author
Edward Renehan Jr. "admitted in court that he had stolen
letters written by George Washington and Abraham Lincoln."

These people, and many more like them, have something in common: all were apparently suffering from bipolar disorder, and their dangerous or illegal behaviors appeared to be a consequence of their illness. In some cases, symptoms were not adequately controlled by medication. Others had stopped taking their medication, or they were abusing alcohol or drugs. Although most people diagnosed with BD do not have such violent, dramatic, or public tragedies, too many do.

Because you and your partner have decided to stick together and fight together for a good life, you will both experience and should talk about these behaviors or the potential for these behaviors together. It is natural for both you and your partner to be embarrassed about bipolar disorder and the symptoms and behaviors it causes, and all too easy in such conversations for each of you to feel overwhelmed and inadequate. Your partner is likely to feel some shame for being ill, some guilt for offensive words spoken or actions taken, and some sense of personal inadequacy for loss of control. You may have similar feelings. Don't reinforce these in your conversations. Arousing negative feelings won't help you work together and find solutions.

In any relationship, we accept limitations and imperfections in our partner, and we work, not toward a perfect relationship, but toward the best interactions possible. Of course you must identify and deal with unacceptable and dangerous behaviors, but it's important to balance talk about illness with talk of your partner's positive attributes and your successes together: "Honey, you're so smart and so great with the kids, and I know you're working hard. If you weren't such a good person, I wouldn't be with you. We've gotten through some pretty bad days in the last few years, and I know we can deal with what's going on now."

Solutions are your partner's responsibility, but this is a team effort. Remind yourself—and your partner—that you, your partner, your doctor, and the rest of your support team are working on problems together.

In this chapter, we offer some coping strategies to help you deal with negative behaviors and spot potentially dangerous situations, and, we hope, keep them from escalating out of control. Despite your best efforts, however, you may not be able to prevent them. If you feel unsafe or seriously threatened at any time, be prepared to leave immediately and call 911.

NEGATIVE BEHAVIORS

Negative behaviors that stop well short of being dangerous can still be troubling and upsetting to both of you. Your partner may exhibit a broad range of bizarre and disturbing symptoms of bipolar disorder. Here are some typical issues that may confront you, along with suggested techniques for coping.

Silence

Sometimes people are so angry, so anxious, or so depressed they can't speak. If your partner stops talking to you entirely, this is not only disconcerting and frustrating but a cause for concern.

Talk with your partner during moments of calm and communication. Explain that not speaking for prolonged periods is disturbing and could be dangerous, at least to the relationship, and is therefore unacceptable; ask for her thoughts and share your ideas on solutions. Relationships in which silences are a substantial factor often benefit from counseling. A good therapist can help you and your partner communicate more effectively.

One very important caveat: *people who are very quiet may be suicidal.* It is always wise to ask about suicidal thoughts if you suspect they may be there.

Blaming

Some people with bipolar disorder tend to blame others when anything goes wrong, even when something is really their own fault—or no one's fault at all. If your partner has a manic grandiosity, she may not be able to accept the idea that something going wrong could possibly be a result of her behavior, so others, including you, must be to blame.

If this happens, take a moment to consider whether you may be at least partly at fault. If so, apologize. If not, you can use a variation of this conversation: "I understand you blame me for . . . , and I know you're upset. I don't agree that I caused the situation, but I'm sorry to know it's given you pain."

Like frequent silences, frequent blaming can seriously disrupt a relationship; but the disruption may be reversible if addressed early. Specifically, this is another behavior that often responds well to professional therapy.

Bullying and Controlling Behavior

Some people who have bipolar disorder can behave in controlling ways, often over matters that seem trivial or even silly. The best tactic is to tune your response to the situation. For example:

You: Sweetie, I think you're getting manic. We need to call your doctor right away or get you to a hospital.
Your partner: I'd never be seen in public with you the way you're dressed now, but I'll go if you wear your red boots.

This kind of situation may involve some unexpressed delusion. You might ask, "Why?" just to check whether something more disturbing is going on. But if the request seems harmless, you might, instead of trying to understand it, simply do what your partner asks for the sake of efficiency in addressing his overall good, and yours.

If your partner is not obviously manic but, for example, insists you sit completely still, or makes similarly unreasonable demands, you might again ask for an explanation ("Why?"). After hearing the explanation, you may be able to find a workable compromise. For example, if your partner is having trouble concentrating, you might point out that even though he might be feeling overwhelmed, it is not reasonable to demand impossible things of you. Perhaps you and he can think of another way to get the tranquility he needs. For example, the two of you might be able to set up space in the house where one of you can go when the other needs to be alone.

At the more extreme end—if your spouse is controlling about what you can wear, what sports the kids can play, who can be your friends, or where and when parties or family events can be held, and offers complex or hard-to-understand reasons—ask for clarification. This can help you figure out whether there is logic there, or just delusion. Respectful but firm feedback on what is or isn't sensible is probably needed, but may not be accepted. This is another instance where outside help from a professional therapist can be extremely valuable.

Religious matters can be among the hardest to handle areas of disagreement and control. Even in the absence of BD, these issues are often deeply emotional, and beliefs and actions are not decided by rational means under every circumstance. The enhancement of emotion and the tendency to read great meaning into events, which are symptoms of BD, can complicate public ceremonies and family get-togethers related to religious holidays or celebrations. Bringing thoughtful clergy or other religious professionals into the discussion can be helpful, if you and your partner trust them.

DANGEROUS AND DESTRUCTIVE BEHAVIOR

"Before the doc got Bill's meds under control, Bill punched a lot of holes in the wall. We can laugh about it now that they're all patched over, but it was kind of scary at the time. It scared him too, once he calmed down."

"My wife is very considerate, except when she slips into a manic episode and starts drinking. Then, watch out! One time, she got angry at the neighbors for parking in what she considered 'her' space on the street, and slashed all of the tires on their car."

It is uncommon for people who have bipolar disorder to damage public property, but it can happen in moments of unusual thinking or extreme agitation. Extensive research has shown that alcohol or other substances are often involved in such situations (another good reason that people who have BD are advised not to drink or to take nonprescribed drugs). Needless to say, this can lead to physical injury, arrests, or lawsuits.

As always, in such situations, your priorities should include keeping yourself, your children, your partner, and any bystanders out of harm's way as best you can, and getting your partner the medication and treatment he needs as *fast* as you can.

Dealing with angry property owners or injured strangers may necessarily fall to you, especially if your partner is too ill to face the consequences of his actions. As in any instance in which one person has clearly wronged another, accepting responsibility, offering apology, and taking prompt action to repair any damage can go a long way. Try not to accuse ("Well, if you hadn't engaged him in an argument . . .") but, rather, to demonstrate a spirit of sympathy, cooperation, and accountability: "I'm so sorry. My husband has not been well. Of course, we'll pay for the damage. Here's where you can reach us."

Responsible behavior is not only called for in such situations but also generally inspires gracious responses in others.

Dealing with Law Enforcement

"When my girlfriend was feeling really, really 'good'—her word—she thought she could get away with anything. Shoplifting was her favorite pastime. I'd come home from work and find the closet full of clothes I knew she hadn't paid for. Finally, she got caught with thousands of dollars worth of jewelry in her bra. I was furious, ready to leave her, so I let her spend the night in jail. Actually, it turned out to be a good thing. A court-ordered psychiatrist thought she might be bipolar, and the judge recommended treatment for her instead of more jail time."

People who have bipolar disorder may, during episodes, engage in unlawful, dangerous, or out-of-control conduct. Worse still, people in the grip of a delusion—like the man in the airport at the beginning of this chapter—have been known to lose their lives in situations in which police have had to act quickly.

Most police officers are well trained to handle dangerous situations, and have knowledge and experience with psychiatric illness; but law enforcement officials cannot always take into account that an individual who is acting "crazy" or dangerously might be a law-abiding, valuable citizen when not in an episode of illness. They cannot always get the information they need to assess whether odd behavior is dangerous or not. If your partner is prone to provocative behavior, it is best if she reduce exposure to public settings, and especially ones that might offer excessive stimulation or stress or bring her into conflict with legal authorities, when symptoms are not in control.

Stay home or seek a supervised treatment setting when illness may lead to behaviors with adverse consequences. It can be wise for someone with BD to carry a card with information stating the diagnosis, listing medication, and providing contact information for the treating doctor to give to police should there be a public incident.

Dangerous Driving

Dangerous driving is a serious matter. If your partner drives recklessly during hypomanic, manic, or depressive episodes— or at any time—you should take over and do as much of the driving as possible. It is appropriate and important to tell a dangerous driver that you are concerned, and to refuse to be a passenger or to allow others to ride in a car driven by that person.

If you don't drive much (or at all), practice or take lessons. Although you may resent having to do more than your share, learning new skills or brushing up on old ones will serve to increase your general competence and freedom. And that's *good*.

When symptoms are quiet, have a no-nonsense talk with your partner. Unsafe drivers put both themselves and others at risk. The sooner you can act to reduce this risk, the better off everyone will be.

LIVING WITH BD

Pam and Mark

Mark's a tense driver, or an *intense* driver, and very impatient and quickly hostile to any driver who drives too slowly, does not signal properly. . . . He is also fairly aggressive, driving faster than I am comfortable with, driving close to other cars, taking corners sharply, pulling out into traffic when the margin of time is not that comfortable.

He also prefers to listen to the radio rather than to carry on a conversation, and when we do talk, he tends to get impatient, cut me off, turn up the radio, curse a driver, flip the bird at another car—sometimes all at once. I, on the other hand, am a "go with the flow" kind of driver, and also a defensive driver. It drives him crazy. The reality is that most people do not like being in the car with him, because he gets revved up, and impatient, and angry, and all his worst qualities come to the surface.

Finally, it got scary. He was driving our eight-year-old daughter and her friend to school, and he tailgated the car in front of him, honking and screaming all the way. He actually cut the guy off—right in front of the school. My daughter and her friend were in tears, the principal called me—it was humiliating, and terrifying. I couldn't believe I'd let him drive like that with her in the car.

Later, when he was calmer, we had a talk. I told him "Never again," and he knows I mean it.

Problems with Reality

People who have bipolar disorder sometimes are given to exaggeration. This may be caused by conceptual problems or outright delusions. If you are concerned about your partner telling tales to friends, acquaintances, and family, you might take comfort in knowing that most people will eventually catch on to the fact that your partner might be entertaining, but not accurate.

Such assessment by others can be hurtful to relationships. It is important, if it is at all possible, to alert your partner to this behavior and to work together to help her recognize and reduce these stories or misrepresentations. Your partner's doctor can assist in evaluating the problem and finding solutions.

HEADING OFF NEGATIVE AND DANGEROUS BEHAVIOR BEFORE IT GETS OUT OF CONTROL

"I used to dread getting phone calls. Before Justin was diagnosed and properly medicated, he was arrested several times for getting in fights. Usually, he was the one getting beaten up, but once, he really hurt a guy and pretty much destroyed a bar he was drinking in. Now, when I see signs he might be working up to something—he's agitated and irritable, he starts picking fights with me, and he gets really loud and embarrassing—I tell him and we do something to stop the escalation."

Most partners of people with BD become experts at spotting the signs of a manic episode. If your partner is given to starting arguments with friends or strangers at social occasions or in public places, you have choices.

Best case: talk beforehand and agree on a signal. When you say the word or make the agreed-on gesture, that tells your partner to stop or disengage from a conversation, or even to go out to the car or to a quiet place immediately and cool off. Of course, this depends on your partner agreeing that he has an illness and that he needs a system to protect himself.

If you haven't reached that point in the relationship and the treatment, concentrate your efforts on doing so. If you have agreed that your partner has an illness, then you and your partner need to go over the danger signs of illness and the circumstances that are most likely to put him at risk. Once you've reviewed those signs, you should be able to agree on an action—usually, this is a personal contact or phrase to alert your partner that he is escalating. This can be as simple as putting your hand on his shoulder, or saying something predetermined to give him an excuse to break off interaction, such as, "Oh, I just realized we need to go talk about arrangements for the weekend" or "That reminded me of something I meant to tell you. Can we take a break and talk?"

Worst case: if your significant other will not adhere, or even agree, to protective measures, insist that the danger of proceeding without plans is too great, and that this is something that needs to be brought up in a meeting with the doctor or other therapists. If you do have a plan, but she seems agitated before a particular event, you must decide between bringing your partner to the event and taking your chances on her behavior, leaving your irritable partner at home, or simply not going. Your partner's safety and comfort should come first. Most events are not worth the consequence of dealing with a dangerous encounter. If you and your partner cannot agree that she will probably be all right at the event, it is usually best not to go.

It might also help to obtain your spouse's permission to tell others, as needed, that she has bipolar disorder (see Chapter Six for a discussion how best to do this). Sharing this information can help explain erratic behavior, elicit understanding and cooperation, and reduce the strain that presenting a "good face" at all times places on both of you.

That said, don't do this without express permission from your partner. Often there are good reasons for keeping this kind of information to oneself, and the choice must belong predominantly to the person directly affected. If the person feels forced into an admission, the relationship can be hurt and the confidence needed to work on other plans for handling illness can be lost.

Try your best to avert problems before they start. Remaining alert to changes in your partner's mood or medication is one essential way of doing this. It's well worth the effort to regularly evaluate how effective you and your partner have been in monitoring the illness and addressing symptoms. Then, if you are not satisfied with your progress, be ready to modify your approach as needed. Set up a schedule together, with or without a therapist, to discuss how well you are doing. Review what you have tried, what has worked, and what has not. Identify issues that are still problems. Go over your options and choose new ways to address whatever is still wrong.

Remember, because violence and other dangerous acts are often associated with drugs and alcohol, your plans should include ways to reduce or eliminate their use. Also, your partner should probably not own or ever carry a weapon. The danger that the weapon might be used during an episode of illness far outweighs any benefit that might be gained from gun ownership.

Domestic Violence

People do not have to be bipolar to engage in domestic violence. However, uncontrolled BD, or BD combined with alcohol or drug abuse, can lead to physical abuse. If you are being abused by your partner, don't hesitate to seek emergency help from friends, family, or the police.

Even if you don't identify with such terms as *battered spouse* or *domestic violence*, but you know that you don't always feel safe with your partner, get counseling from an organization devoted to helping victims of domestic abuse. If you underestimate the threat, you may end up seriously injured or worse. If you feel threatened, there must be a reason for the feeling, and that reason needs to be assessed. It is far more common and more dangerous to procrastinate and not seek help than to discuss the real or perceived threat with your partner and appropriate professionals.

Any violent act or threat is unacceptable in a relationship. This includes punches through a wall, throwing objects in anger, intentionally breaking things, and making verbal threats. **If you are being immediately threatened, call 911.**

You can find information at the National Domestic Violence Hotline: (800) 799-SAFE (7233); TTY: (800) 787-3224; http://www.NDVH.org/.

The National Network to End Domestic Violence (http://www.NNEDV.org/; 800-799-233; TTY: 800-787-3224) offers comprehensive information, as does the National Coalition Against Domestic Violence (http://www.NCADV.org/). You can also search local government pages listings for shelters, women's services, and similar terms.

Domestic violence may affect one out of three women; however, it is not limited to women. By some estimates, one out of every fourteen men will face physical abuse from a spouse or partner at some point. If you are a man who is experiencing domestic violence, check out Stop Abuse For Everyone (SAFE). Its Web site (safe4all.org) provides listings for services in various locations. Not every state or nation is covered, but it is inclusive in terms of the populations it seeks to protect.

Bipolar disorder is an illness. Dealing with it is a balancing act for both of you. You are both allowed, even expected, to have imperfections. Not every inappropriate comment, mood, or behavior is pathological. Learn to understand and forgive yourself as well as your partner. But don't ignore signs of danger, and do talk as openly as you can about your fears and concerns. In the next chapter, we'll look at the intimacy issues that typically plague couples in which at least one member has bipolar disorder.

CHAPTER 10

Sex, Intimacy, and Relationship Issues

In a hypomanic leap, we fly off to New York, whirl through it, have sex continuously, and drink up every bar in the city. . . . We destroy the hotel room. We make a lot of ridiculous promises and grand statements and a hell of a mess. . . . It's taken me exactly two months to leave my husband, find a new playmate, and move across country to my brand new life.

—Marya Hornbacher, *Madness: A Bipolar Life*

Sooner or later, virtually all intimate couples who are living with bipolar disorder experience tensions and troubles around sexual relations. BD tends to affect sexual relationships in particular ways: a partner acting out the hypersexuality of mania is one extreme; a partner who is too depressed or too rooted in self-criticism to have much interest in sexual activity (or whose medication reduces sex drive or performance as one of its side effects) is the other. Sexual intimacy with a depressive partner is limited and may not be possible, and your emotional life with your partner may become painful and alienating.

If you fell in love with your partner when he or she was in a manic or hypomanic mood, you probably made some incorrect assumptions about what your intimate life together would be like. When things change, it's all too easy to blame yourself or your partner. A better idea is to educate yourselves about the relationship between bipolar disorder and sexuality.

HYPERSEXUALITY

A healthy sex drive crosses the line into hypersexuality when sexual behavior becomes clearly excessive or even dangerous. If your partner reaches the level of hypersexuality, he obsesses about sex constantly, may speak often and inappropriately about sex, acts out impulsively, has sex with people he would never want to be with when stable, or feels compelled to have sex frequently, with any partner. This not uncommon symptom of mania can create havoc in relationships.

You may experience this behavior as hurtful and your partner as selfish. But if your relationship is going to have a chance to survive, it's important to understand what hyper-sexuality looks like from the other side.

 LIVING WITH BD

Holly and Tom

Tom and I had been married for ten years—happily, I thought. He was a great lover. Sometimes we'd spend hours and hours making love. Sometimes, he didn't want to be intimate, but who doesn't have those days? I shrugged it off.

Then, over a period of a couple of years, his behavior started to change. He wanted sex at all hours of the day and night. He'd come home hours late from work, and his stories about where he had been didn't add up. Then, in short order, my life turned upside down.

I went to the bank one day and discovered he'd cleaned out our savings. When I confronted him with it, he told me that he had a girlfriend—and not one, but several. They all needed money, and he wanted to provide for them. He seemed to think I would understand this.

I was in shock. He seemed to want me as much as ever—more! How could I not be enough?

I told him if he didn't go to counseling, we were through. He was really upset. He didn't understand what he'd done that was so wrong, but finally he agreed. In counseling, story after story about his infidelities started pouring out. The counselor referred Tom to a psychiatrist and suggested I might want to get my own therapist.

When the psychiatrist diagnosed Tom as bipolar 1, and explained what that meant, things started making more sense—his hypersexuality, and a lot of other moody stuff I'd just sort of ignored over the years.

He's stabilized now, and has told me over and over how terrible he feels about what he's done. At first, I didn't think I'd ever be able to trust him again. I still might not. I've got the bank accounts in my name, and that gives me some peace of mind. But I do love my husband, and we are working on this thing together.

How Hypersexuality Feels to the Person with BD

Bipolar individuals describe this state vividly:

"I couldn't stop thinking about sex. I felt driven to do it with anybody, man or woman, friend or stranger. I was really out of control."

"I wasn't thinking of the consequences of what I was doing. I was overwhelmed by sexual feelings and just kept acting on them."

"I had to have sex every day, sometimes several times a day, and if my wife wasn't around I'd masturbate pretty much all day and all night."

"I felt full of energy and interest in everything, including sex. I was on top of the world and wanted to be on top of everyone else, too."

Affairs Outside the Relationship

Affairs outside the relationship are an all-too-common by-product of hypersexuality. If your partner has had one or more affairs during a manic episode, you probably feel hurt and confused. You may even be entertaining the idea of an extramarital relationship yourself because of your partner's neglect (or as a form of revenge). It is important to remember that your partner is, to some degree, out of control, and not fully responsible for his or her actions.

As sad as it may be to realize it, manic sexual behavior has little or nothing to do with you. Hypersexuality is related to many other symptoms of mania, such as increased energy and heightened interest in all activities, especially the pleasurable ones. The feelings are not under your partner's control, and the actions may not be either, if the feelings become too strong. Remember that impulsivity is also a symptom of mania; the combination of increased sexual drive and decreased control can lead to ill-advised behaviors.

What You Can Do

If you see that your partner is in a hypersexual state, take action. First, alert your partner. Make your partner's treating doctor aware of the problem so that the moods can be stabilized with medication, if appropriate.

If there is evidence that your partner has had an affair, go to a doctor yourself and get checked for sexually transmitted diseases. Insist that your partner do the same. Hypersexuality may not slow down long enough to include precautions like condoms.

Enter into couples therapy. If joint counseling is not an option, make sure to get counseling for yourself. You may also want to investigate support groups for partners. In practice, many couples receive joint and individual counseling while one partner sees a prescribing doctor consistently, sometimes with the spouse, and the other attends regular support group meetings.

LACK OF INTEREST IN SEX OR INTIMACY

In an episode of bipolar depression, all drives, interests, pleasures, and activities tend to decrease. Among these, a lack of interest in sex or intimacy can be as disturbing as a manic sexual episode. Instead of wanting to have sex with you (or anyone else) all the time, your partner seems never to want sex at all. He or she probably does not even want to kiss or touch you.

For the non-BD partner, this can feel like crushing rejection, and you may wonder what you could possibly have done to deserve this kind of treatment. As with hypersexuality, however, it's important to understand what this state is like from the other person's perspective.

 ## LIVING WITH BD

Fran and Dee

Dee would not kiss me. When I would try to hug her, she'd just pull away. If I even touched her during conversation, she'd

(continued)

(*continued*)

shrink back like I'd burned her. It was demoralizing and humiliating. I felt like she hated me. And it was so weird, because most of the time she couldn't get enough of me. She was such an amazing lover. She wanted to do things I'd never heard of, and she looked at me like I was the best candy in the world.

The bipolar diagnosis made sense of her behavior, but it didn't particularly help my emotions. Intellectually, I could see she was on a roller coaster she couldn't control, but what about me? She'd crawl into bed and shun me. She didn't want me anywhere near her. I felt awful.

How Depression Feels to the Person with BD

Here's what people with BD have to say about this state:

"When I'm depressed, I just want to stay in bed and be left alone. Sex is not on my mind. It may be the furthest thing from my mind."

"Kissing my wife was meaningless. There was none of the warmth and rush I used to feel. I felt unmoved and mechanical."

"No interest in sex? Try no interest in anything. I didn't even have the energy to brush my teeth in the morning."

What Can You Do?

As with any symptoms you observe in your partner, if you see signs of depression, including a reduction in sexual behavior, you should alert your partner and talk about it together. However, talk alone will not change the feelings, or lack of them. Pushing your partner too hard or too personally, especially about intimate behavior, may only lead to guilt and tension, which may damage your relationship. Decreased sexual feelings in bipolar depression are part of an episode of illness, and they must be treated as symptoms. This means that you and your partner need to discuss them with a doctor. Good treatment of the depression will usually relieve loss of interest in sex and the other pleasures of life.

Sometimes, loss of interest in sex (or, more commonly, loss of ability to perform intercourse or feel physically aroused) is a side effect of medication. It is not always easy to tell whether such a change is related to illness or its treatment, so it's advisable to check with your partner's doctor. In fact, as a part of monitoring illness and treatment, it should be routine for your partner and his or her doctor to be discussing sexual feelings and activity regularly. Similarly, in your own ongoing evaluation of your partner's illness and your relationship, you and your partner should discuss your feelings about your intimate relationship.

WORKING ON YOUR RELATIONSHIP

Eventually, most couples come to a crossroads: will the partners be able to work together to solve some really tough relationship problems, or will they split up?

Sometimes the partner with BD will leave. It's not uncommon for people with BD to have several marriages, particularly if the disorder is not well stabilized. Often, however, it's the nonbipolar partner who decides the question of whether to stay in the relationship or end it.

You should never stay in a destructive or violent relationship. Beyond that, however, many couples have been able to make their marriage or committed relationship work. (We'll look at these success stories later in the chapter.) First, however, you must decide how committed you are to the person and the relationship.

Seeing What Works in the Relationship

Chances are good that you recognize clearly things that are *wrong* in your relationship. You probably spend enough time thinking about what you'd like to get away from. However, you might not be spending time thinking about what *does* work for you.

Take time to contemplate the positive aspects of your relationship. What do you appreciate about your partner?

"Jess is a photographer, and the way she sees the world . . . well, it's different. When I'm with her, she helps me see things I would ordinarily overlook or not see at all. She just sees the world through a unique frame, and that really expands my world. Hard as life with her is sometimes, I wouldn't want to lose that."

"Ken is so funny. He makes me laugh. Not so much when he's out of control, of course. That can be a nightmare. But when he's stable, he knows how to lighten me up, and I need that."

"Will just 'gets' me like no one else does. I wouldn't give that up for anything."

Marriage as Suicide Prevention

If you're considering leaving your relationship, you will naturally have concerns about your partner's well-being. Will he be able to function on his own? Will she be suicidal if you go? These are the kinds of questions for which you should seek professional guidance.

Generally, it's ill advised to remain in an unhappy relationship as a means of suicide prevention. A person who is suicidal needs professional help. An unhappy relationship needs change. This may mean a change in treatment of an illness causing the unhappiness, a change in the relationship itself, or ending the

---

relationship and moving on. Maintaining a bad, unsatisfying, or unhappy relationship is in no one's best interest.

If you are a mental health professional or in one of the "helping" fields, you may be especially tempted to stay to prevent your partner from taking her own life. But it's unlikely you'll be able to deal with the situation completely on your own in your personal relationship—nor would it be in anyone's best interest for you to do so. Remember the old saying: a doctor who treats himself has a fool for a patient. Wise doctors also don't treat their spouses. Leave that for outside professionals. There are experts who can help you and your partner determine what is wrong with your relationship—it may be different than you think—and help you decide which of many options to choose to improve your lives, whether you stay together or part.

Are You Better Off with or Without Your Partner?

If you realize that you *are* staying in the marriage to keep your partner from committing suicide—and for this reason only—this is definitely something to work on with your counselor or therapist: the relationship you are in is more one of caregiver-patient than of equal or nearly equal partners.

Which leads into the crucial question: Are you better off with or without your partner? This is an interesting question, and one you may not have considered.

- Would you be better off raising your children on your own? Or would the loss of your partner be too difficult for you and your children?
- Does your partner's illness interfere with your own life to the degree that you do not feel as if you have a separate personal life or identity? Or is your partner, despite illness, a benefit to your life and opportunities?

- Do you spend so much time trying to keep your partner stabilized that your own life is in disarray? Or is his or her illness infrequent and tolerable?
- Is your partner's behavior destroying your financial stability and economic future? Or is your partner overall a source of income and the wealth you'll need for retirement?
- Does your partner's illness interfere with your own career or professional possibilities? Or is your partner supportive and helpful, especially when he or she is well?

Consider Taking a Break

If your relationship is so overwhelming that it has taken over your thoughts and has confused, worried, or depressed you, you might need some distance to relax and think. If so, it's a good idea to consider taking a break, formally (a trial separation, in which one of you moves out) or informally (a vacation with friends or time spent alone or with family).

Don't complicate things further by pursuing external romantic relationships during this break time. You should probably also avoid making major changes in your career during this period. Think of it more as a chance to rest, clear your mind, and assess where you want to go from here.

One way to gauge how your life would be if you lived apart is to actually spend time doing so. Approximate, as closely as you can, living however you would after leaving your situation, if you were to do so. Would you, for instance, live alone at first? Under reduced financial circumstances? Consider staying at a hotel, moving back to your parent's home, or subletting for a month or two.

Counseling

If you are considering parting, have not decided, and are not already in couples counseling with a qualified provider, now is the time to start. Make sure, of course, that the therapist you choose is well versed in bipolar disorder.

If your partner refuses to participate, get individual counseling if you are not already doing so. It's important, however, to keep in mind that a counselor who sees only you will hear only your side of the issue, and won't have access to your partner's viewpoint. Some therapists warn that "couples counseling for one" can have disastrous consequences for the counselee's marriage.

If professional counseling is not possible, you might check out online and in-person support groups. Many issues, including relationships, can be usefully discussed in support groups, and others who have struggled with similar circumstances may have good advice. However, beware groups that assign blame to partners or in which others seek to justify their choices by convincing you to do what they did. Helpful discussions include the calm sharing of different points of view, the careful consideration of various options, respect for both parties in a disagreement, and the rejection of simple assumptions as to who is right or wrong.

RECIPES FOR SUCCESS

Yes, there *are* relationship success stories. These long-term couples who have stayed together despite one member's bipolar illness seem to share a number of characteristics.

They Both Take Responsibility

When the ill spouse is able to take responsibility for her own well-being, this takes much of the burden off the non-bipolar partner. Taking responsibility can mean sticking to a medication schedule, arranging psychiatric appointments, shouldering her share of parenting and household responsibilities, and so on.

"We were very fortunate that Camille's medications worked as well as they did. She's been more or less asymptomatic for several years, at this point. She knows she has to stay on her meds, and she's great about doing it. She keeps a chart to make sure she takes them all, and at the correct times, and when we go on trips she always packs extra—just in case we're delayed."

"Rex is very good about apologizing to me when his behavior has gone off the charts for some reason. He may not be able to see it at the time, but afterwards, he takes responsibility for anything he may have said or done that was hurtful or uncalled for."

They Both Stay Vigilant

When only one partner has the responsibility for the other's health, he or she can soon become exhausted with the effort and grow resentful. But when both partners are able to maintain a vigilant watch for warning symptoms, they can act quickly to head off disaster.

"Stew and I agreed long ago that if I ever noticed him getting manic or depressed, I needed to tell him. And if he denied it, it would be okay if I called his doctor to discuss it. For his part, if he feels even the least bit off, he checks in with his doctors. So far, it's worked great for us."

"Edie says she gets a 'feeling' in the pit of her stomach when she's on the verge of hypomania. She always tells me, and we try to nip it in the bud."

They Both Educate Themselves

It's important for both partners to learn as much as possible about bipolar disorder—symptoms, treatments, the latest science. The more knowledge you have, the better able you will be to anticipate problems, take appropriate action, and recognize symptoms as symptoms and not as personal attacks or personality flaws.

"After two years of marriage to Rebecca, I wanted out. I just didn't know how I was going to deal with her peaks and valleys—what did this have to do with *my* life? But as I began to read up on what it meant to be bipolar, what the person with BD was going through, I found that I empathized with her in a way I hadn't before—it's not her fault she's like this. Her brain simply doesn't always work exactly the way she wants."

"I look at Zak's bipolar disorder like it's a chronic illness, which is really what it is—a brain disorder. Would I leave him if he had diabetes? No. But I'd expect him to take his medication and take proper care of his health, and that's exactly what I do with my husband."

They Put the Well Partner in Control of Family Finances

It can be too much to expect your bipolar partner to be in control 100 percent of the time. Instead of blaming your partner, and anguishing over family funds spent during a manic episode, for example, it can be much more effective to take preventive measures. Often, the ill partner grants power of attorney to the well partner in household financial matters.

"Miles is usually pretty stable, but no drug is completely effective. He knows that if he does have a manic episode, it's not inconceivable that he would suddenly sell the house out from under us, or drain our savings to go to Atlantic City. That's why everything we own, including all of our bank accounts, is in my name. And I also have his power of attorney in case anything happens. It's given both of us a bit more peace of mind, and removed a whole layer of issues we don't have to discuss anymore or worry about."

They Stay Healthy

Many long-term couples work together to maintain healthful lifestyles. They each eat a balanced diet, exercise regularly, and get adequate sleep.

"When Rachel stopped drinking coffee and alcohol, our lives took a real turn for the better. She could see that those substances interfered with her medication, and she had a moment of truth. She went on what I called a health kick—going to the gym, cutting out sugar, really taking care of herself. After a while, I realized that it wouldn't hurt if I improved my lifestyle, too. I still drink a cup of coffee in the morning, and have the occasional drink socially. But I've joined her in trying to do the right thing for my body—it's been good for both of us mentally and emotionally, and we've bonded over our daily walks."

They Strategize Ahead of Time

Perhaps most important, partners use periods of wellness to work out plans for times of illness. This implies that they both value the relationship and are willing to work on it together. It also means that if things suddenly go haywire, they have a plan in place that they can implement.

"We've got strategies in place for everything—at least, I think we do. We've got rules for what happens if Sheila feels like she's getting manic or depressed. We've got boundaries I can stick to if she suddenly goes off at me for no reason. We've got appropriate ways to speak to each other, and we practice them. We've got people we can count on to take the kids if that has to happen. And of course we've got all of our emergency numbers up on the wall, and in our wallets."

"Tim's meds seemed fine, he was so stable, and then one day, wham! We were on vacation in the mountains, and he suddenly started talking about what it would be like to drive up the winding road near our hotel and drive straight through the barrier and into the canyon. Thank goodness we'd planned for something like this. I had his doctor's emergency number, the emergency numbers for the county we were in, and the name of the closest mental hospital. I just looked at him and said, 'You know that's not acceptable, right? We've got to get you some help. Get into the car now—and I'm driving.'"

As is true of any relationship, it's vital for couples in a relationship where bipolar disorder is a factor to keep the lines of communication open. Take time to talk. Talk about how both of you think things are going; talk about things that are bothering you. Talk about what works and what *needs* work. Talk early about problems and rough times, before they become habitual or grow to be unmanageable. You can have a good relationship if you can both put in the time, effort, and love.

Even in the best of relationships, however, things can go wrong. That's why it's so important to consider ahead of time how you will cope with an extreme emergency, such as a suicide attempt or hospitalizations. This is the subject of the next chapter.

CHAPTER 11

Suicide Attempts, Hospitalization, and Commitment

I'm going to be a superstar musician, kill myself, and go out in a flame of glory . . .
—Kurt Cobain, rock musician believed to have had bipolar disorder, who committed suicide at age twenty-seven

People in the grip of delusions or mania can sometimes become violent and capable of harming themselves or others, even those they love. It can be terrifying if your partner tries to commit suicide, becomes depressed to the point of near total immobility, or needs immediate psychiatric help for any reason. In cases like these, when your partner is out of control, you will need to take charge.

If you have reason to believe your partner might present a serious threat to anyone, you must act quickly. If your partner is threatening suicide, get in touch with her treating doctor immediately or take your partner to an emergency room. If you think you might be in imminent danger, get yourself and your children to safety right away and call 911.

Anyone who is potentially dangerous should be evaluated at a hospital without delay. Violent acts cannot be reversed and have consequences for health, employment, relationships, and life itself. As always, knowing what to expect ahead of time, and planning for every eventuality, will give your partner the best chance of survival.

PAYING ATTENTION TO SUICIDAL THOUGHTS OR BEHAVIOR

Not everyone who threatens suicide will actually follow through, but you should be aware that the annual average suicide rate for men and women with diagnosed bipolar disorder is estimated to be from ten to more than twenty times that in the general population. And those diagnosed bipolar 2, especially those with agitation or anxiety as part of their symptoms, have higher rates of suicide than individuals diagnosed with most other mental health conditions, including serious depression. It has been estimated that 15 percent of people with BD kill themselves. The threat is very real.

It's crucial that you recognize these warning signs of impending suicide (as given by the National Mental Health Information Center):

• Threatening to hurt or kill oneself or talking about wanting to hurt or kill oneself
• Looking for ways to kill oneself by seeking access to firearms, pills, or other means
• Talking or writing about death, dying, or suicide
• Feeling hopeless
• Feeling rage or uncontrolled anger or seeking revenge

- Acting recklessly or engaging in risky activities—seemingly without thinking
- Feeling trapped—like there's no way out
- Increasing alcohol or drug use
- Withdrawing from friends, family, and society
- Feeling anxious, agitated, or unable to sleep, or sleeping all the time
- Experiencing dramatic mood changes
- Seeing no reason for living or having no sense of purpose in life

When Your Partner Talks About Suicide

If your partner has confided suicidal feelings, try to stay calm. You can tell your spouse she has plenty to live for, or that you and others would be very distressed about her death, but she might not believe it. That disbelief is part of the illness.

If you're concerned that your husband or wife might be thinking about suicide, don't feel afraid to ask. You won't give your partner ideas. Rather, you may save his life. Bring the topic out into the open for discussion. You can simply say, "Are you thinking about killing yourself?" or "Are you thinking about hurting yourself?"

If the answer is "yes," or "maybe," stay calm and get your partner into treatment immediately. Reassure her that you will do what you can to protect her and not allow any such harm to come: "I'm not going to let that happen." "I'm not willing to lose you." Tell your partner you are going to take her to a hospital or her doctor and that you will stay with her until she's safe or feeling better. Getting professional help is critical.

Listen to your partner, but don't criticize, give advice, or talk about your own issues and experiences.

Don't keep a gun in the house. According to many studies, the presence of a firearm greatly increases the probability of suicide (or murder).

Taking Action

If your partner is talking about suicide, take action immediately. Remember: in most cases, people who are considering suicide don't want to die. They want to end their torment.

Get help immediately from one or more of the following resources:

- Your partner's psychiatrist, counselor, or therapist
- Your psychiatrist, counselor, or therapist
- Your local hospital emergency room, a nurse, or a doctor
- 911

You may also call a suicide hotline and put your partner on the phone:

- The National Suicide Prevention Lifeline: 800-273-TALK
- The Samaritans, Suicide Prevention, or your local crisis center
- Your local suicide hotline

If your partner has a plan and means for the suicide attempt, or if the attempt seems imminent, *do not leave her alone—even to call emergency services.* If you can't be there, find someone who can be. Don't leave your partner alone until she is under the care of professionals.

Your loved one's physician and your own doctor, including your family doctor, can also be important resources for assessing and dealing with suicidal thoughts or feelings. Together you can devise a plan for monitoring and addressing destructive thoughts.

Crisis Intervention Story

Here's a story someone who lives with someone with BD told us recently:

> We had two kids in elementary school, and my wife, Lauren, was a stay-at-home mom. I'd only been in my current job for two months. I dropped the kids off at school that morning, because Lauren didn't seem to be able to get out of bed. I guess I knew in the back of my mind that she needed help, but I was too distracted. I certainly wasn't thinking she'd be hospitalized.
>
> Then she called me at work and told me she didn't want to live. Her voice sounded so strange. I called her therapist right away. He told me I needed to get her to the hospital immediately. He called her and kept her talking till I could get there. I drove Lauren to the hospital and she was admitted.
>
> That same day, we had a teacher conference scheduled for my daughter. So I had to leave my wife at the hospital, go to the conference, and then find someone who could take my girls for the day so I could go back to the hospital. It was brutal. We have no family nearby, and I ended up having to ask my neighbor, Sue, for help. She hadn't even known Lauren was bipolar but she was great. Her daughter was in the same grade as our younger girl. She told me not to worry, she'd give them dinner.
>
> On Friday, after I got the girls to school and explained that Mommy was sick and in the hospital, I knew I needed to come up with a plan of action so I could work and our family could function. Although my wife was embarrassed about having people know her situation, I needed help and had to tell a few people for the good of my family.
>
> First, I called the school guidance counselor, and he gave me a contact for afternoon child care.

Then I called my wife's minister. My wife is very active in her church, and this turned out to be a real blessing for us. The minister was a big help. He said that if I couldn't find after-school care, he would meet the kids off the bus and take them to the church. Also, I was able to talk to him about what I was going through, and he gave me his cell number and said I could call any time.

I had a decent enough plan so that I could go to work for the next week or so, and hoped my wife would be out of the hospital soon. Fortunately, she was able to get stabilized in just a few days, at least well enough to come home. I kept up the after-school day care for two weeks after Lauren came home, just to be safe.

It all happened so fast. If it happens again, we'll be more ready. We have some support in place now, and we're both much more careful about responding immediately to any signs that something is wrong.

Calling 911 After a Suicide Attempt

If your partner has made a suicide attempt or is threatening to do so, call 911.

- **Give your address first:** If you call from a landline, the dispatcher may already have this information, but give it anyway. If you call from a cell phone or PBX phone (from inside a workplace, for example), they will not know your location.
- **Then say: "Suicide attempt" or "Threatened suicide," and the means:** For instance, "Suicide attempt with a gun" or "Suicide attempt using Phenobarbital." If it's a drug overdose and a pill bottle is handy, read any information off the label that the dispatcher requests.

- **Remain as calm as possible and stay on the phone:** The 911 operator will lead you through a series of questions while help is being sent. As always when dealing with crisis situations, remain as calm as you can. Stay on the phone until the operator ends the call, and try to keep the line free afterward in case emergency services needs to call.
- **What happens next:** Your partner will be taken to a hospital for an evaluation from the psychiatric doctor on call, and for any treatment that is necessary.

HOSPITALIZATION

If your partner has attempted or is threatening suicide, or is out of control in some other way, hospitalization is often required. Being informed about what this entails is the best way to help your partner through what may be a difficult period of adjustment.

Almost all hospitals—not just psychiatric facilities—can handle mental health emergencies. If your spouse is between doctors, or you're unable to get in touch with his regular provider or backup and you think he is or might present an immediate danger to himself or others, take him to a hospital. Important: if one hospital tries to send you home—even though you know your spouse needs care immediately— hold your ground and ask to see a supervisor. If you make no headway, go to another hospital, not home.

When Is Hospitalization Needed?

For situations that seem concerning, but not desperate—for instance, if your spouse won't get out of bed, or eat, or if he's talking incoherently and rapidly or appears delusional—call his psychiatrist.

If the situation has gone on for longer than twenty-four hours or seems out of control, or you can't reach your partner's doctor, try to persuade him to come to the hospital with you. If you are concerned about safety, call the police to help. They can send an ambulance.

When in doubt, it's better to err on the side of caution. If something seems amiss, call your partner's doctor. Don't worry about whether you're doing everything right. Just getting through the immediate crisis means you are doing what is needed.

Be Prepared

You may not have a lot of time to prepare for your partner's hospitalization, especially if it is in response to a sudden suicide attempt. As upsetting as it may be to think that your partner may someday need to be hospitalized, it is much better to be prepared.

- Have a support group of friends and family you can call on if you need help. Make sure they understand what might be expected of them.
- Gather a few comforting or familiar items for your partner—things as simple as small, unframed photos and soft, warm socks might help your loved one feel more at ease in a stressful situation.
- You will likely be at the hospital with your partner for several hours or more, so include some items for yourself: a cell phone and charger, a small bottle of water, a snack that can travel well, quarters for parking meters, a book to read, an inflatable travel pillow.
- If you need to bring your children along, you'll want to include comfort items for them as well. It will probably be a much better idea, however, if you can enlist a trusted friend, family member, or neighbor to look after them, unless they are grown children.

- Bring a small nonspiral notebook to write down what your spouse's doctors tell you at the hospital, even if you think you'll remember. You'll be grateful later for the written reminders.
- If you hold an office job, you will probably need to explain to your boss or employees that you're caring for a sick spouse. Don't be afraid to ask for the accommodation you need, whether it's emotional, logistical, or both. Generally speaking, burdens grow lighter when shared.

Be prepared to have your possessions searched before your visit. Keep in mind that most psychiatric facilities will look through your partner's belongings and anything you bring in. They have to do this to protect all their patients, including your husband or wife. You will not be permitted to bring things like shoelaces, lighters, or knives; even photo frames, spiral notebooks, shoes, or CD cases may be forbidden, as they can be used in physically harmful ways.

Whether your loved one is in a general hospital or a specialized mental health facility, you might wish to seek out a social worker, or whomever the facility offers for you to talk to. Chances are, you could use a sympathetic ear, advice, and information on hospital policies. Most hospitals also have clergypersons available.

For more information about psychiatric hospitalization, see the following Web page from the Depression and Bipolar Support Alliance: http://www.dbsalliance.org/pdfs/familyhospi talization.pdf.

What to Expect in the Hospital

Hospitalizations—for any condition—are generally short. The average stay for bipolar illness is about ten days. Ideally, patients are evaluated and stabilized, and medication is adjusted or changed. Sometimes they participate in group therapy sessions. Often, patients are checked for other disorders, such as tumors, drug use or exposure, toxins, or hormonal imbalances that can cause behavioral abnormalities.

Typically, your partner would see a psychiatrist briefly in the morning and again later in the day, with some group therapy sessions during the day, if they are appropriate, and in some cases, mild activities and field trips. Mental health facilities often employ teams consisting of a psychiatrist, psychologist, social worker and nurses, and sometimes other professionals as well. Generally, hospital stays are intended to get the patient out of immediate danger and, if needed, begin to adjust medications; subsequent outpatient treatment takes on the more ambitious goal of managing the underlying condition over the long term.

 LIVING WITH BD

Brigitte and John

I didn't know that John had bipolar disorder when I married him, and neither did he. He drank quite a bit. Since we were young and many of our friends drank on weekends, I thought it would pass after we got married. It didn't. Four children and fifteen years later, we began to get an idea of the cause.

When we were young, I mistook his energy and crazy fearlessness for a zest for life. Later, his mood could change like lightning and there would be no way to predict it and no way to deal with it. Then suddenly, the mood would be gone, and he would not understand why the rest of the family was exhausted and feeling unkindly toward him.

He tried to stop drinking as he got older. Sometimes, though, he would just turn up at home drunk, claiming he hadn't been drinking. Many years later, we learned that those times had been dissociative episodes.

The hospitalization came after about twenty years. He began to think his family would be better off without him, and made a suicide attempt: he drank so much alcohol with his medication that he had to be transported by ambulance to a hospital three hours away that would take someone in his condition—he had more than a 0.26 blood alcohol level, and most facilities wouldn't admit patients that drunk.

I cannot explain the pain of driving away from the hospital and leaving him there smelling of whiskey and urine. He was crying because he was not sure what was happening. From the parking lot, I could see him standing in the window of his room. I could not do anything to help him or us. They got him stabilized after three days, and released him.

Fortunately, he has a great provider who's monitored him and his care with his other doctors for years, so he sees that he has his medications. I cannot imagine how we would survive otherwise.

Eventually, we got the diagnosis and the treatment right: Bipolar disorder, medications and therapy. Now, most days are predictable. Our grandkids think their "Pop-pop" is the greatest person in the world, and he feels the same about them. I am glad I'm still here to see this part of his life. If I had left during the worst years, that wouldn't be the case.

John has always loved me and wanted to make things good for me. He feels a horrible guilt for the negative things in our lives. He felt for years that he did not deserve to be loved, and waited every day for me to leave him. That must have been horrifying for him. Of course, he did not share his thoughts with me, and even if he had, he would not have believed my reassurances. He just was not able, with his condition, to understand that I did not blame him for the bipolar.

So here we are, ready to teach a new generation about the family history of bipolar and to help them learn that Pop-pop and Daddy are doing the best they can and we have to do the best we can, too.

Care After Hospitalization

A person who is evaluated as no longer a danger to self or others is discharged. After this, intensive outpatient treatment, often for about two weeks, might be recommended. Clinics, day hospitals, and residential care are all options to consider.

Clinics are traditional outpatient services that offer appointments individually and in groups with psychiatrists, psychologists, social workers, and sometimes occupational therapists. Clinics can offer so-called intensive care, with multiple appointments per week, but more often provide care once a week or once every few weeks.

Day care or *day hospital*, sometimes called *partial hospitalization*, is just what the name implies: patients come in several days a week and receive multiple psychiatric and psychological services, often including groups, each time they come. Usually, these services are for patients recently discharged from a hospital or being treated for an exacerbation of illness not severe enough to require inpatient care but disabling enough to call for a special supportive treatment setting. Patients go home at night. Most commonly, partial hospital care lasts a few weeks.

Residential care, in places often identified as "halfway houses," can last a few days to a few months, or in rare cases, years. It is also for patients who don't require a locked inpatient setting, but do need a supervised place to live, sleep, and receive multiple services.

Caregiver Help

Various community services can take some of the burden off a caregiver—you. These include drop-in centers for people who need help with day-to-day life or work, "clubhouses" with peer-run services and activities, and other resources that can provide assistance with such things as skills training, job placement, social activities and hobbies, or finding treatment. (Peer-run means that those running the clubhouse have psychiatric illnesses themselves.)

If you can afford to, you may want to hire a private helper, such as a professional case manager, who can coordinate care and assist the family by helping the patient make appointments, stay in treatment, and gain new skills.

Anticipating Future Hospitalizations

Even if your partner seems to be stabilized, another hospitalization may be required in the future. Bipolar disorder is an episodic illness. When things are going well, it is easy to forget or deny that symptoms often return. The best way to deal with any emergency is to be prepared. It's difficult to think clearly during a crisis.

When your life has calmed down, write down the things you'll need to know in an emergency: insurance information, the names and phone numbers of your partner's psychiatrist and mental health providers (include after-hours numbers), and local hospitals. Keep the list where you can find it easily. Know which hospital your partner's psychiatrist is affiliated with and what your insurance company will cover.

It's also a good idea to make sure that your house number is clearly readable from the street, in case police or ambulance personnel need to find it.

IF YOUR PARTNER NEEDS TO BE COMMITTED

Commitment—confining a patient to a hospital or mental health facility against her wishes—is not easy, and for very good reasons: throughout history and in many countries

Talking with Children About a Parent's Hospitalization

Children of any age are likely to feel concerned about the well-being of their parent and about whether their own needs will continue to be met. Do your best to reassure them, without making promises you can't keep.

When talking with younger children, keep it matter-of-fact: "Daddy needs to spend some time in the hospital. The doctors there are giving him care to help him feel better. In the meantime, Aunt Betty will be helping me take good care of you."

If you have young children, you'll need someone to care for them while you're busy dealing with hospital matters. Family members, other parents, or trusted neighbors can be a good resource.

Follow these guidelines to reassure your children during your partner's hospitalization:

- Maintain frequent contact with your children. If you and your children are not in the same place, call at least once a day if possible.
- Text messages, IMs, and other personal communication will help your children feel more connected and less anxious.
- If it's necessary for the kids to sleep away from home, make sure to pack familiar and comforting items, such as favorite toys or photos.

Older children may want to help. This can be good for all of you—but take care to remember that an older child is, nonetheless, a child. Fostering a spirit of cooperation ("While Dad's in the hospital, it would be very helpful if you could start dinner and watch Joey when he gets home from school") is good. Confiding your darkest worries or expecting too much in the way of adult responsibilities is not.

currently, people seen as troublemakers (who may not have been ill) have been involuntarily committed, sometimes for long periods, to get them off the streets. In the United States, laws passed in the 1960s and 1970s gave more rights and protections to the patient—and rightly so.

Today, the chief criterion for psychiatric confinement is the patient's "being dangerous" to self or to others. If your partner fits this criterion, you might find that you need to think about committing him or her. Family members can—and, in certain circumstances, *should*—take the patient to an emergency room or psychiatric facility if he is obviously in trouble. But only a doctor or judge can legally *commit* a patient to a hospital. (Patients who are committed do not lose legal rights. For example, their wills remain valid.)

Protocol varies from state to state, but ordinarily such involuntary confinement is initiated by a doctor or by a call to the police, who are authorized to bring potential patients to a local psychiatric ward.

The Commitment Process

After your partner goes through an initial "hold," which in many places is seventy-two hours for observation and treatment, you may need to participate in a commitment hearing. You and the treating doctors will be expected to answer questions and defend your reasoning. Commitment hearings are private (that is, details are not made available to the public) and often take place in hospital conference rooms. The patient receives legal counsel or even free representation if needed. This process is designed to protect the rights of the patient.

For the most part, laws governing involuntary commitment vary according to state. In many cases, they also vary by individual community. There may be a second seventy-two-hour hold and then a lengthier hearing to determine whether long-term treatment is needed. If you live outside the United States, you may find local laws applicable to this situation are quite different from those mentioned previously.

Most individuals who are ill accept treatment. But don't be afraid to work with the hospital and doctors if commitment is needed. It can save a life.

Guardianship

Rarer than commitment—and more complex—is an arrangement called guardianship. In guardianship, responsibility for decision making with regard to an individual who is unable to care for himself is given to a legally designated person. This is usually a spouse or close family member, but can sometimes be an independent third party. The decisions a guardian can make include those in the areas of personal health, safety, welfare, and, if appropriate, property and finances.

Generally, a judge appoints the guardian and specifies his or her specific powers. The judge will retain some oversight to ensure protection of the rights and care of the individual. If you're considering guardianship, speak with a lawyer or the psychiatric hospital's liaison.

Suicide and hospitalization are not the only difficult situations for those close to someone with bipolar disorder. Many issues surrounding BD—including the possibility that there are other bipolar family members—also put the families of these individuals under a great deal of stress. In the final chapter, we'll look at some healthy ways to deal with these other family issues.

CHAPTER 12

Family Matters

My wife Roberta . . . is quiet, strong. She knows the school calendar and remembers the mortgage. She leaves me notes in the morning. She says the kids will be fine, that they take after her side on this, my family's disease. They'll have, she said, the best of both worlds and I want to believe her.

But I want to be ready. I've seen both my parents drown in the sickness. I've seen my brother sink down. I've denied my own madness and I've loved it almost to death. All my life I've heard my family blame each other, some devil, some church, genetics and shrinks. We come up for air but never swim home. We're ashamed and afraid of our minds. I want to believe my wife and not worry. I want to get strong and show my kids how. I want my family fearless and proud.

—David Lovelace, *Scattershot: My Bipolar Family*

Bipolar disorder doesn't just affect the person diagnosed with BD, and doesn't just affect you, the partner: it affects everyone in your family, directly or indirectly. And because bipolar disorder has a genetic component, there is a possibility that members of your partner's family are also struggling with BD, and that your children may now or someday be dealing with BD in their own lives. There is even the possibility that you also have BD, or are dealing with other psychological and emotional issues.

As we noted in the opening chapter, psychiatric disorders—including depression, anxiety, BD, and other disorders—are very common. In addition, many of us have a tendency to emotional instability, even if we don't have a diagnosable disorder. This is part of being human; it is just more extreme in families where there is BD.

HEALTHY FAMILY GUIDELINES

Helping your partner manage her illness is important, but it should not rule your life or your family's life. Most people with bipolar disorder can have full lives, including family lives.

In many ways, the tools that will help your partner maintain stability are the same ones that help any family live and grow in healthy ways. However, these tools are even more important where bipolar disorder is involved, because symptoms and episodes of illness can be brought out by physical and emotional stress or unhealthy habits. Help your partner pay special attention to the following areas. (All of this advice is good for you, too, as it will help you maintain your physical and emotional health.)

Physical Health

- Each of you should have a medical doctor who knows you well. Have regular checkups and treat all illnesses that arise.
- Maintain a healthy weight.

- Eat regular meals, with a diverse diet of healthy foods. Nutritional deficiency may increase the risk for an episode of illness.
- Exercise regularly—ideally, every day at the same time. Regular activity rhythms have been shown to protect against bipolar episodes. Setting aside a time to exercise together with your partner can be effective for both of you, as you are more likely to keep your commitment if you work out together.
- Have a sleep routine that includes regular hours for going to bed and waking up, and get the right amount of sleep, usually a good eight hours a night. Maintaining a consistent daily rhythm of activities and sleep has been shown to help stabilize BD. It has also been shown to increase energy and alertness and improve mood in those without an illness.
- Avoid alcohol for your partner and limit it for yourself. Avoid all "recreational" drugs. They will destabilize your partner's illness and they will put you at risk for emotional problems.

Emotional Health

- Set healthy expectations and boundaries for work and in relationships and stick to them.
- Learn and practice effective communication techniques with family, friends, and colleagues.
- Plan regular enjoyable and relaxing activities, and make sure you all take regular vacations and time off from work.
- Have a sport or hobby you each enjoy, and make special time to practice it.
- Learn a technique for relaxation—meditation, reading, painting, music, or another activity that helps you be calm.

Family Health

- Try to eat meals at a regular time and together as a family.
- Structure time and activities together so that everyone feels a part of the family and knows what to expect of one another.
- Include your partner as a full member of the family, not as the "sick" one.
- Plan regular family and individual meetings to discuss how everyone is doing. Address everyone's concerns, and let everyone feel heard.

Being Prepared

- Post all emergency phone numbers—911, your partner's doctors, the local hospital—where everyone old enough to use them can see them.
- Have a plan, and make sure everyone in the family knows what he or she is supposed to do in case of emergency, including specific plans for action if your partner is confused, agitated, or unresponsive.
- Make sure your children know they can and should tell you if they see something that worries them. (Make sure your partner knows the children are part of this plan.) Try to create an environment where everyone, not just your partner, can share their concerns about others or their own problems with others in the family.
- Make sure your children have a safe place to stay and people to care for them if that should become necessary. Make sure, too, that your children know there is a plan for their safety and comfort, should you have to leave the house in an emergency to take care of your partner.

WHEN YOUR PARTNER IS NOT THE ONLY ONE IN THE FAMILY WHO IS BIPOLAR

You may have another bipolar member of your family—parents, aunts or uncles, brothers or sisters—in addition to your partner. If they have been diagnosed and are dealing effectively with their own issues, that's probably all that should concern you.

Frequently, however, other family members have undiagnosed illness. Their behavior may be sending up red flags for you, but they may be unaware that their problems point to BD, may be in denial that anything is wrong at all, and may actively resist and resent any efforts on your part to help them.

Except under special circumstances of guardianship (see Chapter Eleven), you can't exercise control over another adult. If your parent or sibling, or those of your partner, are or could be bipolar, think about whether a discussion would prove valuable. This may be easiest if you know the person well and know how best to approach him or her. Anything you say may be taken as a criticism, so phrasing is important.

It may be best to try to get into a discussion with your Aunt Jessie, for example, about the time she started yelling at the bride about her choice of dress during a family wedding. You might tell her how upsetting that was to other guests, and asking for her point of view on what happened that day. Your aunt may not be aware that she did something that worried others, and may even feel comfortable enough to tell you that she often feels unwell or out of control. If she is open to the possibility that she may have a problem, she will be more likely to accept advice and seek help.

If she cannot see or accept that she may have a problem, that could be part of the illness, and no amount of explaining or examples from you will change her mind. Rather, it will probably just make your relationship more tense. Nonetheless you needn't accept the relationship on these terms. You don't have to agree with anything your relatives say that seems "wrong" to you, and you don't have to look the other way at behaviors you feel are inappropriate. You can calmly state your observations or disagreements, or set limits in ways that make your position clear, without engaging in arguments or undue criticism. You can let them know you care and that you want to have a good relationship and these are the reasons you are telling them what you see. Some of the communication techniques we discussed in Chapter Eight may be useful here.

If the spouse of someone in your partner's family who appears to have untreated bipolar disorder approaches you for advice, proceed carefully. For example, if your sister-in-law tells you she is worried about her husband, your partner's brother, ask if she and her partner have discussed this possibility. If they haven't, ask why not. Encourage them to make this an open issue if they can. Ask if they have educated themselves about bipolar disorder and how to deal with it. If not, encourage them to do so. Sharing your experiences can be useful, if your partner knows that you are doing so. Offering to help, yourself, is generous, but be careful about taking on additional responsibility, unless you have the time and emotional resources to handle more obligations.

Try not to engage in conversations behind someone's back, if those conversations could include the person you are trying to help. If you must give advice about someone else, remember that you are getting information from only one person—not from the person about whom you are talking. Avoid the temptation to engage in merely criticizing the person you are discussing, as opposed to seeking ways to understand and help that person. Keep reminding the person who is seeking your advice that there are ways to bring up most issues with his or her partner. It is important not to play the role of expert, but to advise, or help, the person who has approached you to get professional aid in dealing with problems related to illness.

WHEN YOU HAVE A BIPOLAR CHILD

If you suspect your child has BD, do your best to get a thorough evaluation and an accurate diagnosis. As criteria for the diagnosis and treatment of bipolar disorder in children are controversial, even among experts, an appropriate evaluation may include a second opinion. Bipolar shares some similarities with other disorders, and children, especially, can easily be misdiagnosed and either inappropriately or inadequately medicated. Also, children misbehave, are moody, have unusual thoughts, and have sleep problems—all symptoms of BD—for many reasons. Just because your partner is bipolar doesn't mean your child is too. Nonetheless, the risk of bipolar disorder is higher in a child of a parent with bipolar disorder. You should be alert to the possibility that inappropriate thoughts or behaviors or problems in school or relationships could be due to BD and could be treatable.

If your child has been diagnosed as having BD, educate yourself as much as possible about childhood bipolar disorder. Symptoms and treatment are not exactly the same as in adults. There is a great deal of literature for parents of bipolar children, including books, Web sites, and online forums that provide information and emotional support. Especially for the treatment of children, it is important to find a psychiatrist who is an expert both in childhood disorders and in bipolar disorder. In addition to the general advice in Chapter Three about finding a psychiatrist, the resources listed in "Youth Mental Health Organizations" are also useful.

Early Onset BD

Childhood bipolar disorder—known as *early onset* BD—is associated with more pronounced symptoms and more frequent mood swings (throughout life) than BD that first becomes evident in adults.

Youth Mental Health Organizations

Active Minds on Campus
  (202) 332-9595
  http://www.activemindsoncampus.org/

American Academy for Child and Adolescent Psychiatry
  (202) 966-7300
  http://www.aacap.org/

Child and Adolescent Bipolar Foundation
  http://www.bpkids.org/

Federation of Families for Children's Mental Health
  http://www.ffcmh.org/

Juvenile Bipolar Research Foundation
  (866) 333-JBRF (5273)
  E-mail: info@jbrf.org
  http://www.bpchildresearch.org/

Although much is being studied and discovered, there are still many unknowns regarding BD in childhood and much controversy about treatment, especially with regard to medication. Learn as much as you can about children and medicine, and about the particular medication your doctor recommends. If your child is on medication, learn about and keep an eye out for troubling or dangerous side effects—not only at the beginning of treatment but also after any dosage changes or additions—and stay in touch with your child's doctor regularly.

If you do have a bipolar child, or children, it would probably be wise to talk with your child's teachers. You may need to make special arrangements to accommodate the effects of medications, reduce stresses, or handle difficult behaviors.

There are no perfect children; psychiatric disorders are common in children, as they are in adults. The U.S. Surgeon General estimated that at least one out of five children has a psychiatric disorder serious enough to require treatment, so your child is not alone. Also, there is unprecedented awareness today about bipolar disorders in children as well as in teens and adults. There are effective medications and treatments. Many people with BD are successful in life, and many successful people have BD. Your child may be one of them. You can help by providing your continuing love and support, just as you would give any child.

Should You Have Children If One or Both of You Has Bipolar Disorder?

Bipolar disorder tends to run in families. If you are planning to have children and this possibility is a matter of concern for you, have a talk with your family doctor or ob-gyn. He or she may suggest genetic counseling. In the end, however, the decision is up to you and your partner. Among the factors you need to consider are the following:

- Bipolar disorder has a genetic component (see Chapter One), and your children would be at increased risk of illness. Are both you and your partner prepared for that possibility?
- Many people who have BD are good parents. But parenting is stressful. If you are trying hard to manage the stress in your life, you should factor this into your decision.
- Pregnancy can precipitate the first or new symptoms of bipolar disorder. So plan the timing of pregnancies with your psychiatrist, make sure your ob-gyn knows if you have BD, and watch for symptoms.
- A bipolar woman who is pregnant will need to be carefully monitored by her doctor. Certain medications can harm a fetus, and these will most likely need to be adjusted or replaced.

The Bipolar Teen

Adolescence is difficult for everyone, and bipolar teenagers in particular often get into substance abuse, sexual exploration, and other risky behaviors. If you're the parent of a bipolar teen, you'll need to keep a particular eye out for these dangers. Keep the lines of communication open: talk to your children and, above all, listen. Seek support from other parents of bipolar children and teenagers.

Teenagers are not adults. They still need effective parenting: to support them and to set boundaries and help them keep to their limits. You are responsible for them. Even when they tell you to get out of their lives and you are tempted to do just that, remember: you are the parent and the responsible adult.

Find a provider who will counsel your teen privately but will also maintain appropriate and responsive contact with you, the parents. Be involved. Monitor your teen's behavior and stay in direct contact with his or her doctor.

LIVING WITH BD

Martin's Family

My older daughter, Vanessa, was diagnosed with bipolar disorder at fifteen after she tried to kill herself. Even though my wife had been diagnosed some years before, and we knew this was a possibility, we were taken by surprise. We just hadn't seen signs that anything was wrong.

Our youngest daughter, Rayanne, took it really hard, but we made sure she got counseling—in fact, the whole family was in counseling—and things seemed more or less okay with her. She got good grades, had a nice boyfriend, and got into a good college.

She loved the dorm, loved school, and we relaxed. For a few months, everything seemed to be going great for her. Then all hell broke loose. She called, hysterical, in the middle of the night, saying she'd been kicked out and we had to come get her right away. We later found out she had acquired a reputation as the wildest girl in the dorm—she'd get drunk, she'd get stoned, and she'd sleep with everybody. Boys, her professors, townies . . . She never went to class. We were stunned. She'd always been a quiet girl, a good student.

My wife and I were devastated. I guess being away from home, without structure, and with the pressures of school . . . it was just too much for Rayanne.

She moved back home so we could try to get this thing under control. Both our daughters are doing okay now, fingers crossed. We all feel really fortunate that our daughters are both alive and trying their best to cope with this thing.

WHEN YOU HAVE PROBLEMS OF YOUR OWN

It is possible, if not probable, that you brought your own problems to your relationship with a bipolar partner. Epidemiologic studies suggest that it's not unlikely that you suffer from some level of depression or anxiety, for instance. It's not just a matter of these conditions being common; people with mood disorders are also more likely than average to marry other persons with mood disorders, including BD.

Although, for some, caregiving and busy-ness provide needed focus, if you tend toward depression, caring for a partner with BD probably won't enhance your overall spirits. The same holds for anxiety and related disorders: bipolar symptoms and behaviors can make ordinary life much more trying for everyone in the household. Make sure your own condition is evaluated and treated, with medication if needed. Learning cognitive-behavioral and relaxation techniques to deal with your own stress can help you calm anxiety and cope with the pressure and worry of having a bipolar partner.

WHEN BOTH OF YOU ARE BIPOLAR

It's not uncommon for both members of a couple to have bipolar disorder. The most likely reason seems to be a phenomenon that epidemiologists and other scientists call *assortative mating*—that is, we tend to gravitate toward others who are like ourselves.

If you and your partner both have bipolar disorder, you'll have some advantages and some disadvantages. One big advantage, of course, is that if you learn about your illness and your options, you can help each other: reminders about medication and appointments, or suggestions about calling the therapist may less likely be met with resistance than if only one of you were ill.

You can also watch for, and help minimize, your partner's "triggers." You'll possess an inherent understanding of the challenges, and may know almost exactly how your partner feels, especially if you have the same type of bipolar disorder. (Because bipolar 1 is less prevalent than bipolar 2, it's less likely that both members of a couple will be bipolar 1.) Forgiveness and understanding might also come easier.

Your situation also holds potential disadvantages. If you are both ill at the same time, you may urge each other into dangerous behavior without the safety of a well partner to caution or stop you.

During episodes of illness, the ill partner will be less equipped to look after the other partner, and vice versa.

At the same time, as noted earlier, you're in an excellent position to help your partner. You can, ideally, take turns, one watching out for the other during episodes of illness. It is therefore more likely for you than for other couples that each of you does his or her fair share in the relationship. Make sure, however, that you have others to rely on, and plans for what to do if both of you are ill at the same time.

It is not wrong for both of you to see the same doctor if you both have the same illness. Often, this is the doctor who prescribes your medications. However, you will probably each benefit from also having someone you *don't* share to talk with about your problems. Often, this is a professional therapist.

LIVING WITH BD
Marylou and Tim

My husband, Tim, is bipolar, but he's not my first bipolar relationship. My last two boyfriends before him were bipolar too. I actually went years without realizing this, or even thinking about it. I was used to butting heads with my boyfriends, yelling and screaming about stuff, dealing with their addictions and depressions . . . and I was really hooked in to what I saw as the good times, what I later came to realize was the manic sexual energy and a life of exciting, sometimes dangerous, activities.

Then I noticed that when I tried to talk to my friends about my relationship woes, they'd give me some pretty strange looks. Apparently, not everyone had to deal with this kind of stuff. Not all women are attracted to extreme men.

Tim started seeing a psychiatrist, and got medicated, and started to get stabilized. Then, *I* was upset! He seemed kind of boring to me. At about that point, I could see I needed my own therapist.

In therapy, some stuff came out, and I realized that my mom had probably been bipolar—not diagnosed, of course—and my granddad as well. After many years of exposure to mania, this kind of behavior just seemed normal to me. I didn't know it wasn't ordinary. Turns out, I may be bipolar, too, and that may explain some of what I want and choose to do.

My therapist is helping me understand why I have such a drive to keep repeating this kind of relationship. I'm learning a lot about myself. Some of it is scary, but I feel like I'm finally getting some control over what I do. I thought about leaving

(*continued*)

(*continued*)
Tim, but then I thought, now? When we're both actually starting
to get better? I truly love my husband. We just fit together. I'm
determined to make it work. Continuing couples therapy,
medication for both of us, trying to talk instead of argue . . .
whatever it takes.

WHY DID YOU END UP WITH A BIPOLAR PARTNER?

Just as some bipolar qualities represent the worst that one can
bring to relationships, others are positive and can attract
powerfully during courtship. To wit: bipolar illness can
make your partner daring, sexy, animated, successful, confi-
dent, optimistic, fascinating, and more.

People who suffer from bipolar disorder also tend toward
high vitality (at least sometimes), creativity, and even brilliance. Some partners describe an almost magical quality to
their bipolar spouses' behavior or conversation, at least during
times when they are not experiencing deep depressions. Many
people who are bipolar exhibit abundant charm, humor, or
"the gift of gab" when they are manic; and during depressive
phases, they may be perceived as having a kind of "romantic"
broodiness.

Are certain kinds of people more likely than others to end
up with bipolar partners? As of now, no one knows for
certain—but, based on observation, it certainly seems so.
Some people, as we've said elsewhere, are attracted to the
charm and excitement and confidence of a person in a manic
or hypomanic mood. Others romanticize depression, seeing in
it a sign of a deeply sensitive nature rather than an indication
and symptom of unhappiness or pain. And if you have been
raised by parents (diagnosed or undiagnosed) with bipolar or
other emotional or mental disorders, then unpredictable, wild,

and even dangerous behavior may seem like the norm. This is what you expect from a relationship; and when you get it, it may feel satisfying and rewarding or comfortable and familiar—a feeling of "coming home."

Often, partners of people who have bipolar disorder are smart and creative themselves; it is therefore not hard to understand why they would appreciate those qualities in others. One thing's a practical certainty: chances are, the bipolar person in your life is, at the very least, interesting.

You Are Not Alone: Online Resources for Bipolar Disorder

The most important thing to remember is that you are not alone. There are many other people in your position, and a number of excellent online services (listed here in alphabetical order) are available to help you out:

- Bipolar Significant Others: http://bpso.org/
- Bipolar Support.org: http://bipolarsupport.org/
- BP Hope (part of *BP Magazine*): http://bphope.com/
- The Depression and Bipolar Support Alliance: DBSAlliance.org
- Harbor of Refuge (online support and information): http://www.harbor-of-refuge.org/
- Healthy Place (online mental health community): Healthyplace.com/Communities/Bipolar/index.asp
- The Mayo Clinic: MayoClinic.com
- McLean Hospital: Mclean.Harvard.edu
- McLean support information page: Mclean.Harvard.edu/education/consumers/groups.php
- The National Alliance on Mental Illness: NAMI.org
- The National Institute of Mental Health: nimh.nih.gov
- Pendulum.org
- WebMd.com

The future holds great promise for our growing understanding of bipolar disorder and for helping the individuals who live with it. But you don't have to wait for the future to begin living a healthy, constructive, hopeful life with the bipolar person in your life: your partner. We hope this book has given you a deeper understanding of bipolar disorder in general, the role it plays in each of your lives, and the support that is out there for both of you as you work together to live with BD.

We urge you to continue to educate yourself about bipolar disorder. Continue to ask your partner's doctor about new medications and other therapies that may soon become available. Keep asking questions of doctors and therapists about any concerns you may have. Encourage your partner to work on new coping skills, and continue to work on your own. Care for yourself so that you can care for your partner. Don't neglect to get appropriate support or to take time for yourself. Keep up caring communications between you and your partner. Treat this illness with determination. You *can* live a healthy, productive, and loving life with someone who is living with bipolar disorder.

APPENDIX

Excerpts from the *DSM-IV-TR* Diagnostic Criteria for Bipolar Disorder

P lease note: The following excerpts from the *DSM-IV-TR* include information about major manic and depressive episodes. They do not include the specific diagnostic criteria for bipolar 1 and bipolar 2 or other forms of bipolar disorder. This information is available in the original source.

MAJOR DEPRESSIVE EPISODE

Episode Features

The essential feature of a Major Depressive Episode is a period of at least two weeks during which there is either depressed mood or the loss of interest or pleasure in nearly all activities.

Reprinted with permission from the *Diagnostic and Statistical Manual of Mental Disorders, Text Revision, Fourth Edition* (Copyright 2000). American Psychiatric Association.

In children and adolescents, the mood may be irritable rather than sad. The individual must also experience at least four additional symptoms drawn from a list that includes changes in appetite or weight, sleep, and psychomotor activity; decreased energy; feelings of worthlessness or guilt; difficulty thinking, concentrating, or making decisions; or recurrent thoughts of death or suicidal ideation, plans, or attempts. To count toward a Major Depressive Episode, a symptom must either be newly present or must have clearly worsened compared with the person's pre-episode status. The symptoms must persist for most of the day, nearly every day, for at least two consecutive weeks. The episode must be accompanied by clinically significant distress or impairment in social, occupational, or other important areas of functioning. For some individuals with milder episodes, functioning may appear to be normal but requires markedly increased effort.

The mood in a Major Depressive Episode is often described by the person as depressed, sad, hopeless, discouraged, or "down in the dumps" (Criterion A1). In some cases, sadness may be denied at first, but may subsequently be elicited by interview (e.g., by pointing out that the individual looks as if he or she is about to cry). In some individuals who complain of feeling "blah," having no feelings, or feeling anxious, the presence of a depressed mood can be inferred from the person's facial expression and demeanor. Some individuals emphasize somatic complaints (e.g., bodily aches and pains) rather than reporting feelings of sadness. Many individuals report or exhibit increased irritability (e.g., persistent anger, a tendency to respond to events with angry outbursts or blaming others, or an exaggerated sense of frustration over minor matters). In children and adolescents, an irritable or cranky mood may develop rather than a sad or dejected mood. This presentation should be differentiated from a "spoiled child" pattern of irritability when frustrated.

Loss of interest or pleasure is nearly always present, at least to some degree. Individuals may report feeling less interested in hobbies, "not caring anymore," or not feeling any enjoyment in activities that were previously considered pleasurable (Criterion A2). Family members often notice social withdrawal or neglect of pleasurable avocations (e.g., a formerly avid golfer no longer plays, a child who used to enjoy soccer finds excuses not to practice). In some individuals, there is a significant reduction from previous levels of sexual interest or desire.

Appetite is usually reduced, and many individuals feel that they have to force themselves to eat. Other individuals, particularly those encountered in ambulatory settings, may have increased appetite and may crave specific foods (e.g., sweets or other carbohydrates). When appetite changes are severe (in either direction), there may be a significant loss or gain in weight, or, in children, a failure to make expected weight gains may be noted (Criterion A3).

The most common sleep disturbance associated with a Major Depressive Episode is insomnia (Criterion A4). Individuals typically have middle insomnia (i.e., waking up during the night and having difficulty returning to sleep) or terminal insomnia (i.e., waking too early and being unable to return to sleep). Initial insomnia (i.e., difficulty falling asleep) may also occur. Less frequently, individuals present with oversleeping (hypersomnia) in the form of prolonged sleep episodes at night or increased daytime sleep. Sometimes the reason that the individual seeks treatment is for the disturbed sleep.

Psychomotor changes include agitation (e.g., the inability to sit still, pacing, handwringing; or pulling or rubbing of the skin, clothing, or other objects) or retardation (e.g., slowed speech, thinking, and body movements; increased pauses before answering; speech that is decreased in volume inflection, amount, or variety of content, or muteness) (Criterion

A5). The psychomotor agitation or retardation must be severe enough to be observable by others and not represent merely subjective feelings.

Decreased energy, tiredness, and fatigue are common (Criterion A6). A person may report sustained fatigue without physical exertion. Even the smallest tasks seem to require substantial effort. The efficiency with which tasks are accomplished may be reduced. For example, an individual may complain that washing and dressing in the morning are exhausting and take twice as long as usual.

The sense of worthlessness or guilt associated with a Major Depressive Episode may include unrealistic negative evaluations of one's worth or guilty preoccupations or ruminations over minor past failings (Criterion A7). Such individuals often misinterpret neutral or trivial day-to-day events as evidence of personal defects and have an exaggerated sense of responsibility for untoward events. For example, a realtor may become preoccupied with self-blame for failing to make sales even when the market has collapsed generally and other realtors are equally unable to make sales. The sense of worthlessness or guilt may be of delusional proportions (e.g., an individual who is convinced that he or she is personally responsible for world poverty). Blaming oneself for being sick and for failing to meet occupational or interpersonal responsibilities as a result of the depression is very common and, unless delusional, is not considered sufficient to meet this criterion.

Many individuals report impaired ability to think, concentrate, or make decisions (Criterion A8). They may appear easily distracted or complain of memory difficulties. Those in intellectually demanding academic or occupational pursuits are often unable to function adequately even when they have mild concentration problems (e.g., a computer programmer who can no longer perform complicated but previously manageable tasks). In children, a precipitous drop in grades may reflect poor concentration. In elderly individuals with a Major Depressive Episode, memory difficulties may be the chief complaint and may be mistaken for early signs of a dementia ("pseudodementia"). When the Major Depressive Episode is successfully treated, the memory problems often fully abate. However, in some individuals, particularly elderly persons, a Major Depressive Episode may sometimes be the initial presentation of an irreversible dementia.

Frequently there may be thoughts of death, suicidal ideation, or suicide attempts (Criterion A9). These thoughts range from a belief that others would be better off if the person were dead, to transient but recurrent thoughts of committing suicide, to actual specific plans of how to commit suicide. The frequency, intensity, and lethality of these thoughts can be quite variable. Less severely suicidal individuals may report transient (one- to two-minute), recurrent (once or twice a week) thoughts. More severely suicidal individuals may have acquired materials (e.g., a rope or a gun) to be used in the suicide attempt and may have established a location and time when they will be isolated from others so that they can accomplish the suicide. Although these behaviors are associated statistically with suicide attempts and may be helpful in identifying a high-risk group, many studies have shown that it is not possible to predict accurately whether or when a particular individual with depression will attempt suicide. Motivations for suicide may include a desire to give up in the face of perceived insurmountable obstacles or an intense wish to end an excruciatingly painful emotional state that is perceived by the person to be without end.

A diagnosis of a Major Depressive Episode is not made if the symptoms meet criteria for a Mixed Episode (Criterion B). A Mixed Episode is characterized by the symptoms of both a Manic Episode and a Major Depressive Episode occurring nearly every day for at least a one-week period.

The degree of impairment associated with a Major Depressive Episode varies, but even in mild cases, there must be either clinically significant distress or some interference in social, occupational, or other important areas of functioning (Criterion C). If impairment is severe, the person may lose the ability to function socially or occupationally. In extreme cases, the person may be unable to perform minimal self-care (e.g., feeding or clothing self) or to maintain minimal personal hygiene.

A careful interview is essential to elicit symptoms of a Major Depressive Episode. Reporting may be compromised by difficulties in concentrating, impaired memory, or a tendency to deny, discount, or explain away symptoms. Information from additional informants can be especially helpful in clarifying the course of current or prior Major Depressive Episodes and in assessing whether there have been any Manic or Hypomanic Episodes. Because Major Depressive Episodes can begin gradually, a review of clinical information that focuses on the worst part of the current episode may be most likely to detect the presence of symptoms. The evaluation of the symptoms of a Major Depressive Episode is especially difficult when they occur in an individual who also has a general medical condition (e.g., cancer, stroke, myocardial infarction, diabetes). Some of the criterion items of a Major Depressive Episode are identical to the characteristic signs and symptoms of general medical conditions (e.g., weight loss with untreated diabetes, fatigue with cancer). Such symptoms should count toward a Major Depressive Episode except when they are clearly and fully accounted for by a general medical condition. For example, weight loss in a person with ulcerative colitis who has many bowel movements and little food intake should not be counted toward a Major Depressive Episode. On the other hand, when sadness, guilt, insomnia, or weight loss are present in a person with a recent myocardial infarction, each symptom would count toward a Major Depressive Episode because these are not clearly and fully accounted for by the physiological effects of a myocardial infarction. Similarly, when symptoms are clearly due to mood-incongruent delusions or hallucinations (e.g., a thirty-pound weight loss related to not eating because of a delusion that one's food is being poisoned), these symptoms do not count toward a Major Depressive Episode.

By definition, a Major Depressive Episode is not due to the direct physiological effects of a drug of abuse (e.g., in the context of Alcohol Intoxication or Cocaine Withdrawal), to the side effects of medications or treatments (e.g., steroids), or to toxin exposure. Similarly, the episode is not due to the direct physiological effects of a general medical condition (e.g., hypothyroidism) (Criterion D). Moreover, if the symptoms begin within two months of the loss of a loved one and do not persist beyond these two months, they are generally considered to result from Bereavement (see p. 740), unless they are associated with marked functional impairment or include morbid preoccupation with worthlessness, suicidal ideation, psychotic symptoms, or psychomotor retardation (Criterion E).

Associated Features and Disorders

Associated descriptive features and mental disorders. Individuals with a Major Depressive Episode frequently present with tearfulness, irritability, brooding, obsessive rumination, anxiety, phobias, excessive worry over physical health, and complaints of pain (e.g., headaches or joint, abdominal, or other pains). During a Major Depressive Episode, some individuals have Panic Attacks that occur in a pattern that meets criteria for Panic Disorder. In children, separation anxiety may occur. Some individuals note difficulty in intimate relationships, less satisfying social interactions, or difficulties in sexual functioning (e.g., anorgasmia in women or erectile dysfunction in men). There may be marital problems (e.g., divorce), occupational problems (e.g., loss of job), academic problems (e.g., truancy, school failure), Alcohol or Other Substance Abuse, or increased utilization of medical services. The most serious consequence of a Major Depressive Episode is attempted or completed suicide. Suicide risk is especially high for individuals with psychotic features, a history of previous suicide attempts, a family history of completed suicides, or concurrent substance use. There may also be an increased rate of premature death from general medical conditions. Major Depressive Episodes often follow psychosocial stressors (e.g., the death of a loved one, marital separation, divorce). Childbirth may precipitate a Major Depressive Episode, in which case the specifier With Postpartum Onset is noted (see p. 422).

The pathophysiology of a Major Depressive Episode may involve a dysregulation of a number of neurotransmitter systems, including the serotonin, norepinephrine, dopamine, acetylcholine, and gamma-aminobutyric acid systems. There is also evidence of alterations of several neuropeptides, including corticotrophin-releasing hormone. In some depressed individuals, hormonal disturbances have been observed, including elevated glucocorticoid secretion (e.g., elevated urinary free cortisol levels or dexamethasone nonsuppression of plasma cortisol) and blunted growth hormone, thyroid-stimulating hormone, and prolactin responses to various challenge tests.

Functional brain imaging studies document alterations in cerebral blood flow and metabolism in some individuals, including increased blood flow in limbic and paralimbic regions and decreased blood flow in the lateral prefrontal cortex. Depression beginning in late life is associated with alterations in brain structure, including periventricular vascular changes. None of these changes are present in all individuals in a Major Depressive Episode, however, nor is any particular disturbance specific to depression.

Specific Culture, Age, and Gender Features

Culture can influence the experience and communication of symptoms of depression. Underdiagnosis or misdiagnosis can be reduced by being alert to ethnic and cultural specificity in the presenting complaints of a Major Depressive Episode. For example, in some cultures, depression may be experienced largely in somatic terms, rather than with sadness or guilt. Complaints of "nerves" and headaches (in Latino and Mediterranean cultures), of weakness, tiredness, or "imbalance" (in Chinese and Asian cultures), of problems of the "heart" (in Middle Eastern cultures), or of being "heartbroken" (among Hopi) may express the depressive experience. Such presentations combine features of the Depressive, Anxiety, and Somatoform Disorders. Cultures also may differ in judgments about the seriousness of experiencing or expressing dysphoria (e.g., irritability may provoke greater concern than sadness or withdrawal).

Culturally distinctive experiences (e.g., fear of being hexed or bewitched, feelings of "heat in the head" or crawling sensations of worms or ants, or vivid feelings of being visited by those who have died) must be distinguished from actual hallucinations or delusions that may be part of a Major Depressive Episode, With Psychotic Features. It is also imperative that the clinician not routinely dismiss a symptom merely because it is viewed as the "norm" for a culture.

The core symptoms of a Major Depressive Episode are the same for children and adolescents, although there are data that suggest that the prominence of characteristic symptoms may change with age. Certain symptoms such as somatic complaints, irritability, and social withdrawal are particularly common in children, whereas psychomotor retardation, hypersomnia, and delusions are less common in prepuberty than in adolescence and adulthood. In prepubertal children, Major Depressive Episodes occur more frequently in conjunction with other mental disorders (especially Disruptive Behavior Disorders, Attention-Deficit Disorders, and Anxiety Disorders) than in isolation. In adolescents, Major Depressive Episodes are frequently associated with Disruptive Behavior Disorders, Attention-Deficit Disorders, Anxiety Disorders, Substance-Related Disorders, and Eating Disorders. In elderly adults, cognitive symptoms (e.g., disorientation, memory loss, and distractibility) may be particularly prominent.

Women are at significantly greater risk than men to develop Major Depressive Episodes at some point during their lives, with the greatest differences found in studies conducted in the United States and Europe. This increased differential risk emerges during adolescence and may coincide with the onset of puberty. Thereafter, a significant proportion of women report a worsening of the symptoms of a Major Depressive Episode several days before the onset of menses. Studies indicate that depressive episodes occur twice as frequently in women as in men. See the corresponding sections of the texts for Major Depressive Disorder (p. 372), Bipolar I Disorder (p. 385), and Bipolar II Disorder (p. 394) for specific information on gender.

Course

Symptoms of a Major Depressive Episode usually develop over days to weeks. A prodromal period that may include anxiety symptoms and mild depressive symptoms may last for weeks to months before the onset of a full Major Depressive Episode. The duration of a Major Depressive Episode is also variable. An untreated episode typically lasts four months or longer, regardless of age at onset. In a majority of cases, there is complete remission of symptoms, and functioning returns to the premorbid level. In a significant proportion of cases (perhaps 20%–30%), some depressive symptoms insufficient to meet full criteria for a Major Depressive Episode may persist for months to years and may be associated with some disability or distress (in which case the specifier In Partial Remission may be noted; p. 412). Partial remission following a Major Depressive Episode appears to be predictive of a similar pattern after subsequent episodes. In some individuals (5%–10%), the full criteria for a Major Depressive Episode continue to be met for two or more years (in which case the specifier Chronic may be noted; see p. 417).

Differential Diagnosis

A **Substance-Induced Mood Disorder** is distinguished from a Major Depressive Episode by the fact that a substance (e.g., a drug of abuse, a medication, or a toxin) is judged to be etiologically related to the mood disturbance (see p. 405). For example, depressed mood that occurs only in the context of withdrawal from cocaine would be diagnosed as Cocaine-Induced Mood Disorder, With Depressive Features, With Onset During Withdrawal.

In elderly persons, it is often difficult to determine whether cognitive symptoms (e.g., disorientation, apathy, difficulty concentrating, memory loss) are better accounted for by a **dementia** or by a Major Depressive Episode. A thorough medical evaluation and an evaluation of the onset of the disturbance, temporal sequencing of depressive and cognitive symptoms, course of illness, and treatment response are helpful in making this determination. The premorbid state of the individual may help to differentiate a Major Depressive Episode from a dementia. In a dementia, there is usually a premorbid history of declining cognitive function, whereas the individual with a Major Depressive Episode is much more likely to have a relatively normal premorbid state and abrupt cognitive decline associated with the depression.

Major Depressive Episodes with prominent irritable mood may be difficult to distinguish from **Manic Episodes with irritable mood** or from **Mixed Episodes.** This distinction requires a careful clinical evaluation of the presence of manic symptoms. If criteria are met for both a Manic Episode and a Major Depressive Episode (except for the two-week duration) nearly every day for at least a one-week period, this would constitute a Mixed Episode.

Distractibility and low frustration tolerance can occur in both **Attention-Deficit/Hyperactivity Disorder** and a Major Depressive Episode; if the criteria are met for both, Attention-Deficit/Hyperactivity Disorder may be diagnosed in addition to the Mood Disorder. However, the clinician must be cautious not to overdiagnose a Major Depressive Episode in children with Attention-Deficit/Hyperactivity Disorder whose disturbance in mood is characterized by irritability rather than by sadness or loss of interest.

A Major Depressive Episode that occurs in response to a psychosocial stressor is distinguished from **Adjustment Disorder With Depressed Mood** by the fact that the full criteria for a Major Depressive Episode are not met in Adjustment Disorder. After the loss of a loved one, even if depressive symptoms are of sufficient duration and number to meet criteria for a Major Depressive Episode, they should be attributed to **Bereavement** rather than to a Major Depressive Episode, unless they persist for more than two months or include marked functional impairment, morbid preoccupation with worthlessness, suicidal ideation, psychotic symptoms, or psychomotor retardation.

Finally, **periods of sadness** are inherent aspects of the human experience. These periods should not be diagnosed as a Major Depressive Episode unless criteria are met for severity (i.e., five out of nine symptoms), duration (i.e., most of the day, nearly every day for at least two weeks), and clinically significant distress or impairment. The diagnosis **Depressive Disorder Not Otherwise Specified** may be appropriate for presentations of depressed mood with clinically significant impairment that do not meet criteria for duration or severity.

Criteria for Major Depressive Episode

A. Five (or more) of the following symptoms have been present during the same two-week period and represent a change from previous functioning; at least one of the symptoms is either (1) depressed mood or (2) loss of interest or pleasure.
   Note: Do not include symptoms that are clearly due to a general medical condition, or mood-incongruent delusions or hallucinations.
   1. depressed mood most of the day, nearly every day, as indicated by either subjective report (e.g., feels sad or empty) or observation made by others (e.g., appears tearful). **Note:** In children and adolescents, can be irritable mood.
   2. markedly diminished interest or pleasure in all, or almost all, activities most of the day, nearly every day (as indicated by either subjective account or observation made by others)

3. significant weight loss when not dieting, or weight gain (e.g., a change of more than 5% of body weight in a month), or decrease or increase in appetite nearly every day.
   Note: In children, consider failure to make expected weight gains.
4. insomnia or hypersomnia nearly every day
5. psychomotor agitation or retardation nearly every day (observable by others, not merely subjective feelings of restlessness or being slowed down)
6. fatigue or loss of energy nearly every day
7. feelings of worthlessness or excessive or inappropriate guilt (which may be delusional) nearly every day (not merely self-reproach or guilt about being sick)
8. diminished ability to think or concentrate, or indecisiveness, nearly every day (either by subjective account or as observed by others)
9. recurrent thoughts of death (not just fear of dying), recurrent suicidal ideation without a specific plan, or a suicide attempt or a specific plan for committing suicide

B. The symptoms do not meet criteria for a Mixed Episode.
C. The symptoms cause clinically significant distress or impairment in social, occupational, or other important areas of functioning.
D. The symptoms are not due to the direct physiological effects of a substance (e.g., a drug of abuse, a medication) or a general medical condition (e.g., hypothyroidism).
E. The symptoms are not better accounted for by Bereavement, i.e., after the loss of a loved one, the symptoms persist for longer than two months or are characterized by marked functional impairment, morbid preoccupation with worthlessness, suicidal ideation, psychotic symptoms, or psychomotor retardation.

MANIC EPISODE

Episode Features

A Manic Episode is defined by a distinct period during which there is an abnormally and persistently elevated, expansive, or irritable mood. This period of abnormal mood must last at least one week (or less if hospitalization is required) (Criterion A). The mood disturbance must be accompanied by at least three additional symptoms from a list that includes inflated self-esteem or grandiosity, decreased need for sleep, pressure of speech, flight of ideas, distractibility, increased involvement in goal-directed activities or psychomotor agitation, and excessive involvement in pleasurable activities with a high potential for painful consequences. If the mood is irritable (rather than elevated or expansive), at least four of the above symptoms must be present (Criterion B). The symptoms do not meet criteria for a Mixed Episode, which is characterized by the symptoms of both a Manic Episode and a Major Depressive Episode occurring nearly every day for at least a one-week period (Criterion C). The disturbance must be sufficiently severe to cause marked impairment in social or occupational functioning or to require hospitalization, or it is characterized by the presence of psychotic features (Criterion D). The episode must not be due to the direct physiological effects of a drug of abuse, a medication, other somatic treatments for depression (e.g., electroconvulsive therapy or light therapy), or toxin exposure. The episode must also not be due to the direct physiological effects of a general medical condition (e.g., multiple sclerosis, brain tumor) (Criterion E).

The elevated mood of a Manic Episode may be described as euphoric, unusually good, cheerful, or high. Although the person's mood may initially have an infectious quality for the uninvolved observer, it is recognized as excessive by those who know the person well. The expansive quality of the mood is characterized by unceasing and indiscriminate enthusiasm for interpersonal, sexual, or occupational interactions. For example, the person may spontaneously start extensive conversations with strangers in public places, or a salesperson may telephone strangers at home in the early morning hours to initiate sales. Although elevated mood is considered the prototypical symptom, the predominant mood disturbance may be irritability, particularly when the person's wishes are thwarted. Lability of mood (e.g., the alternation between euphoria and irritability) is frequently seen.

Inflated self-esteem is typically present, ranging from uncritical self-confidence to marked grandiosity, and may reach delusional proportions (Criterion B1). Individuals may give advice on matters about which they have no special knowledge (e.g., how to run the United Nations). Despite lack of any particular experience or talent, the individual may embark on writing a novel or composing a symphony or seek publicity for some impractical invention. Grandiose delusions are common (e.g., having a special relationship to God or to some public figure from the political, religious, or entertainment world).

Almost invariably, there is a decreased need for sleep (Criterion B2). The person usually awakens several hours earlier than usual, feeling full of energy. When the sleep disturbance is severe, the person may go for days without sleep and yet not feel tired.

Manic speech is typically pressured, loud, rapid, and difficult to interrupt (Criterion B3). Individuals may talk nonstop, sometimes for hours on end, and without regard for others' wishes to communicate. Speech is sometimes characterized by joking, punning, and amusing irrelevancies. The individual may become theatrical, with dramatic mannerisms and singing. Sounds rather than meaningful conceptual relationships may govern word choice (i.e., clanging). If the person's mood is more irritable than expansive, speech may be marked by complaints, hostile comments, or angry tirades.

The individual's thoughts may race, often at a rate faster than can be articulated (Criterion B4). Some individuals with Manic Episodes report that this experience resembles watching two or three television programs simultaneously. Frequently there is flight of ideas evidenced by a nearly continuous flow of accelerated speech, with abrupt changes from one topic to another. For example, while talking about a potential business deal to sell computers, a salesperson may shift to discussing in minute detail the history of the computer chip, the industrial revolution, or applied mathematics. When flight of ideas is severe, speech may become disorganized and incoherent.

Distractibility (Criterion B5) is evidenced by an inability to screen out irrelevant external stimuli (e.g., the interviewer's tie, background noises or conversations, or furnishings in the room). There may be a reduced ability to differentiate between thoughts that are germane to the topic and thoughts that are only slightly relevant or clearly irrelevant.

The increase in goal-directed activity often involves excessive planning of, and excessive participation in, multiple activities (e.g., sexual, occupational, political, religious) (Criterion B6). Increased sexual drive, fantasies, and behavior are often present. The person may simultaneously take on multiple new business ventures without regard for the apparent risks or the need to complete each venture satisfactorily. Almost invariably, there is increased sociability (e.g., renewing old acquaintances or calling friends or even strangers at all hours of the day or night), without regard to the intrusive, domineering, and demanding nature of these interactions. Individuals often display psychomotor agitation or restlessness by pacing or by holding multiple conversations simultaneously (e.g., by telephone and in person at the same time). Some s write a torrent of letters on many different topics to blic figures, or the media.

siveness, unwarranted optimism, grandiosity, and poor judgment often lead to an imprudent involvement in pleasurable activities such as buying sprees, reckless driving, foolish business investments, and sexual behavior unusual for the person, even though these activities are likely to have painful consequences (Criterion B7). The individual may purchase many unneeded items (e.g., twenty pairs of shoes, expensive antiques) without the money to pay for them. Unusual sexual behavior may include infidelity or indiscriminate sexual encounters with strangers.

The impairment resulting from the disturbance must be severe enough to cause marked impairment or to require hospitalization to protect the individual from the negative consequences of actions that result from poor judgment (e.g., financial losses, illegal activities, loss of employment, assaultive behavior). By definition, the presence of psychotic features during a Manic Episode constitutes marked impairment in functioning (Criterion D).

Symptoms like those seen in a Manic Episode may be due to the direct effects of antidepressant medication, electroconvulsive therapy, light therapy, or medication prescribed for other general medical conditions (e.g., corticosteroids). Such presentations are not considered Manic Episodes and do not count toward the diagnosis of Bipolar I Disorder. For example, if a person with recurrent Major Depressive Disorder develops manic symptoms following a course of antidepressant medication, the episode is diagnosed as a Substance-Induced Mood Disorder, With Manic Features, and there is no switch from a diagnosis of Major Depressive Disorder to Bipolar I Disorder. Some evidence suggests that there may be a bipolar "diathesis" in individuals who develop manic-like episodes following somatic treatment for depression. Such individuals may have an increased likelihood of future Manic, Mixed, or Hypomanic Episodes that are not related to substances or somatic treatments for depression. This may be an especially important consideration in children and adolescents.

Associated Features and Disorders

Associated descriptive features and mental disorders. Individuals with a Manic Episode frequently do not recognize that they are ill and resist efforts to be treated. They may travel impulsively to other cities, losing contact with relatives and caretakers. They may change their dress, makeup, or personal appearance to a more sexually suggestive or dramatically flamboyant style that is out of character for them. They may engage in activities that have a disorganized or bizarre quality (e.g., distributing candy, money, or advice to passing strangers). Gambling and antisocial behaviors may accompany the Manic Episode. Ethical concerns may be disregarded even by those who are typically very conscientious (e.g., a stockbroker inappropriately buys and sells stock without the clients' knowledge or permission; a scientist incorporates the findings of others). The person may be hostile and physically threatening to others. Some individuals, especially those with psychotic features, may become physically assaultive or suicidal. Adverse consequences of a Manic Episode (e.g., involuntary hospitalization, difficulties with the law, or serious financial difficulties) often result from poor judgment and hyperactivity. When no longer in the Manic Episode, most individuals are regretful for behaviors engaged in during the Manic Episode. Some individuals describe having a much sharper sense of smell, hearing, or vision (e.g., colors appear very bright). When catatonic symptoms (e.g., stupor, mutism, negativism, and posturing) are present, the specifier With Catatonic Features may be indicated.

Mood may shift rapidly to anger or depression. Depressive symptoms may last moments, hours, or, more rarely, days. Not uncommonly, the depressive symptoms and manic symptoms occur simultaneously. If the criteria for both a Major Depressive Episode and a Manic Episode are prominent every day for at least one week, the episode is considered to be a Mixed Episode. As the Manic Episode develops, there is often a substantial increase in the use of alcohol or stimulants, which may exacerbate or prolong the episode.

Specific Culture, Age, and Gender Features

Cultural considerations that were suggested for Major Depressive Episodes are also relevant to Manic Episodes. Manic Episodes in adolescents are more likely to include psychotic features and may be associated with school truancy, antisocial behavior, school failure, or substance use. A significant minority of adolescents appear to have a history of long-standing behavior problems that precede the onset of a frank Manic Episode. It is unclear whether these problems represent a prolonged prodrome to Bipolar disorder or an independent disorder. See the corresponding sections of the texts for Bipolar I Disorder and Bipolar II Disorder for specific information on gender.

Course

The mean age at onset for a first Manic Episode is the early twenties, but some cases start in adolescence and others start after age fifty years. Manic Episodes typically begin suddenly, with a rapid escalation of symptoms over a few days. Frequently, Manic Episodes occur following psychosocial stressors. The episodes usually last from a few weeks to several months and are briefer and end more abruptly than Major Depressive Episodes. In many instances (50%–60%), a Major Depressive Episode immediately precedes or immediately follows a Manic Episode, with no intervening period of euthymia. If the Manic Episode occurs in the postpartum period, there may be an increased risk for recurrence in subsequent postpartum periods and the specifier With Postpartum Onset is applicable.

Differential Diagnosis

A Manic Episode must be distinguished from a **Mood Disorder Due to a General Medical Condition.** The appropriate diagnosis would be Mood Disorder Due to a General Medical Condition if the mood disturbance is judged to be the direct physiological consequence of a specific general medical condition (e.g., multiple sclerosis, brain tumor, Cushing's syndrome). This determination is based on the history, laboratory findings, or physical examination. If it is judged that the manic symptoms are not the direct physiological consequence of the general medical condition, then the primary Mood Disorder is recorded on Axis I (e.g., Bipolar I Disorder) and the general medical condition is recorded on Axis III (e.g., myocardial infarction). A late onset of a first Manic Episode (e.g., after age fifty years) should alert the clinician to the possibility of an etiological general medical condition or substance.

A **Substance-Induced Mood Disorder** is distinguished from a Manic Episode by the fact that a substance (e.g., a drug of abuse, a medication, or exposure to a toxin) is judged to be etiologically related to the mood disturbance. Symptoms like those seen in a Manic Episode may be precipitated by a drug of abuse (e.g., manic symptoms that occur only in the context of intoxication with cocaine would be diagnosed as Cocaine-Induced Mood Disorder, With Manic Features, With

Onset During Intoxication). Symptoms like those seen in a Manic Episode may also be precipitated by antidepressant treatment such as medication, electroconvulsive therapy, or light therapy. Such episodes are also diagnosed as Substance-Induced Mood Disorders (e.g., Amitriptyline-Induced Mood Disorder, With Manic Features; Electroconvulsive Therapy-Induced Mood Disorder, With Manic Features). However, clinical judgment is essential to determine whether the treatment is truly causal or whether a primary Manic Episode happened to have its onset while the person was receiving the treatment.

Manic Episodes should be distinguished from **Hypomanic Episodes.** Although Manic Episodes and Hypomanic Episodes have an identical list of characteristic symptoms, the disturbance in Hypomanic Episodes is not sufficiently severe to cause marked impairment in social or occupational functioning or to require hospitalization. Some Hypomanic Episodes may evolve into full Manic Episodes.

Major Depressive Episodes with prominent irritable mood may be difficult to distinguish from Manic Episodes with irritable mood or from **Mixed Episodes.** This determination requires a careful clinical evaluation of the presence of manic symptoms. If criteria are met for both a Manic Episode and a Major Depressive Episode nearly every day for at least a one-week period, this would constitute a Mixed Episode.

Attention-Deficit/Hyperactivity Disorder and a Manic Episode are both characterized by excessive activity, impulsive behavior, poor judgment, and denial of problems. Attention-Deficit/Hyperactivity Disorder is distinguished from a Manic Episode by its characteristic early onset (i.e., before age seven years), chronic rather than episodic course, lack of relatively clear onsets and offsets, and the absence of abnormally expansive or elevated mood or psychotic features.

Criteria for Manic Episode

A. A distinct period of abnormally and persistently elevated, expansive, or irritable mood, lasting at least one week (or any duration if hospitalization is necessary).
B. During the period of mood disturbance, three (or more) of the following symptoms have persisted (four if the mood is only irritable) and have been present to a significant degree:
   1. inflated self-esteem or grandiosity
   2. decreased need for sleep (e.g., feels rested after only three hours of sleep)
   3. more talkative than usual or pressure to keep talking
   4. flight of ideas or subjective experience that thoughts are racing
   5. distractibility (i.e., attention too easily drawn to unimportant or irrelevant external stimuli)
   6. increase in goal-directed activity (either socially, at work or school, or sexually) or psychomotor agitation
   7. excessive involvement in pleasurable activities that have a high potential for painful consequences (e.g., engaging in unrestrained buying sprees, sexual indiscretions, or foolish business investments)
C. The symptoms do not meet criteria for a Mixed Episode.
D. The mood disturbance is sufficiently severe to cause marked impairment in occupational functioning or in usual social activities or relationships with others, or to necessitate hospitalization to prevent harm to self or others, or there are psychotic features.
E. The symptoms are not due to the direct physiological effects of a substance (e.g., a drug of abuse, a medication, or other treatment) or a general medical condition (e.g., hyperthyroidism).

Note: Manic-like episodes that are clearly caused by so-matic antidepressant treatment (e.g., medication, electro-convulsive therapy, light therapy) should not count toward a diagnosis of Bipolar I Disorder.

Associated Features and Disorders

Associated descriptive features and mental disorders. Completed suicide occurs in 10%–15% of individuals with Bipolar I Disorder. Suicidal ideation and attempts are more likely to occur when the individual is in a depressive or mixed state. Child abuse, spouse abuse, or other violent behavior may occur during severe Manic Episodes or during those with psychotic features. Other associated problems include school truancy, school failure, occupational failure, divorce, or episodic anti-social behavior. Bipolar Disorder is associated with Alcohol and other Substance Use Disorders in many individuals. Individuals with earlier onset of Bipolar I Disorder are more likely to have a history of current alcohol or other substance use problems. Concomitant alcohol and other substance use is associated with an increased number of hospitalizations and a worse course of illness. Other associated mental disorders include Anorexia Nervosa, Bulimia Nervosa, Attention-Deficit/Hyperactivity Disorder, Panic Disorder, and Social Phobia.

Familial Pattern

First-degree biological relatives of individuals with Bipolar I Disorder have elevated rates of Bipolar I Disorder (4%–24%), Bipolar II Disorder (1%–5%), and Major Depressive Disorder (4%–24%). Those individuals with Mood Disorder in their first-degree biological relatives are more likely to have an earlier age at onset. Twin and adoption studies provide strong evidence of a genetic influence for Bipolar I Disorder.

NOTES

Chapter 1

Epigraph: Kay Redfield Jamison, *An Unquiet Mind* (New York: Vintage Books/Random House, 1995), 6.

What Are the Symptoms of Bipolar Disorder? National Institute of Mental Health, http://www.nimh.nih.gov/health/publications/bipolar-disorder/complete-index.shtml.

Chapter 2

Epigraph: Anthony Storr, http://www.bipolar-lives.com/quotes-on-bipolar.html.

Quotation of Nellie Bly: excerpt from *Ten Days in a Madhouse* (New York: Norman L. Munro, 1887), 18, from http://digital.library.upenn.edu/women/bly/madhouse/madhouse.html.

A Very Partial List of Famous People Who Are, Were, or May Have Been Bipolar: Bipolar disorder is a relatively recent diagnostic term, so it is impossible to say with certainty that this or that historical personage was diagnosed as bipolar. The people on this list, however, are generally believed to have been bipolar, or have been diagnosed with the disorder. Many similar lists are available by online search.

Chapter 3

Epigraph: John Morgan, with Stephen A. Shoop, "Mariette Hartley Triumphs over Bipolar Disorder," http://www.talentdevelop. com/bipolar.html.

Bipolar People May Need *Help* to Get Help: National Institute of Mental Health, http://www.nimh.nih.gov/health/publications/ bipolar-disorder/how-can-individuals-and-families-get-help-for-bipolar-disorder.shtml.

Chapter 4

Epigraph: Carrie Fisher, http://www.brainyquote.com/quotes/ authors/c/carrie_fisher.html.

Chapter 5

Epigraph: Lizzie Simon, *My Bipolar Road Trip in 4-D* (New York: Washington Square Press, 2003), backmatter.

Chapter 6

Epigraph: Andy Behrman, "Electroboy Looks Back: 10-Year Diagnosis Anniversary," updated May 16, 2006, About.com http://bipolar.about.com/od/electroboy/a/040616_andy.htm.

Chapter 7

Epigraph: Terri Cheney, *Manic: A Memoir* (New York: Harper Paperbacks, 2009), 78.

Chapter 8

Epigraph: Jane Thompson, *Sugar and Salt: My Life with Bipolar Disorder* (Bloomington, IN: Authorhouse, 2006), 114.

Chapter 9

Epigraph: Kay Redfield Jameson, in Robert Crawford, *Contemporary Poetry and Contemporary Science* (Oxford University Press, 2006), 194.

Information on Jayson Blair from http://bipolar.about.com/cs/crime/a/jaysonblair.htm.

Information on Edward Renehan Jr. from Jay Akasi, "Illness and Crime: A Difficult Connection to Prove," *New York Sun*, June 23, 2008, http://www.nysun.com/health-fitness/bipolar-illness-and-crime-a-difficult-connection/80491/.

Chapter 10

Epigraph: Marya Hornbacher, *Madness: A Bipolar Life* (New York: Houghton Mifflin, 2008), 94.

Chapter 11

Epigraph: Kurt Cobain, http://www.bipolar-lives.com/quotes-on-bipolar.html.

"Not everyone who threatens suicide . . . twenty times that in the general population": Leslie Citrome and Joseph F. Goldberg, "Bipolar Disorder Is a Potentially Fatal Disease," http://www.postgradmed.com/issues/2005/02_05/comm_citrome.htm.

Warning signs of impending suicide: U.S. Department of Health and Human Services, Substance Abuse and Mental Health Services Administration National Mental Health Information Center, http://mentalhealth.samhsa.gov/publications/allpubs/walletcard/engwalletcard.asp.

Chapter 12

Epigraph: David Lovelace, *Scattershot: My Bipolar Family* (New York: Dutton Adult, 2008), 29.

RESOURCES

BIPOLAR AND MENTAL HEALTH ORGANIZATIONS

Academy of Cognitive Therapy
(267) 350-7683
E-mail: info@academyofct.org
http://www.academyofct.org/

American Psychiatric Association (APA)
http://www.psych.org/

APA District branch information:
http://onlineapa.psych.org/listing/

American Psychological Association
(800) 374-2721
http://www.apa.org/

Depression and Bipolar Support Alliance
(800) 826-3632
http://www.dbsalliance.org/

Families for Depression Awareness
(781) 890-0220
http://www.familyaware.org/

Mental Health America
(800) 969-6642
http://www.mentalhealthamerica.net/

NARSAD (The Mental Health Research Association)
(800) 829-8289
E-mail: info@narsad.org
http://www.narsad.org/

National Alliance on Mental Illness
Helpline: (800) 950-6264
http://www.nami.org/

National Institute of Mental Health
http://www.nimh.nih.gov/

National Mental Health Awareness Campaign
(800) 273-8255
http://www.nostigma.org/

MENTAL HEALTH SERVICES AND MEDICAL RESOURCES

SAMHSA's Mental Health Services Locator
http://mentalhealth.samhsa.gov/databases/
Comprehensive information about mental health services and resources throughout the United States.

Center for Mental Health Services (CMHS) Knowledge Exchange Network (KEN)
(800) 789-2647

http://mentalhealth.samhsa.gov/
Part of the SAMHSA Health Information Network, which provides the latest information on the prevention and treatment of mental and substance use disorders.

HealthLinks
http://www.healthlinks.net/
This Web site is a portal service for health care professionals and consumers to assist in locating medical and health care information, resources, services, and practitioners on the Web.

The Mayo Clinic
http://www.mayoclinic.com/

McLean Hospital
(800) 333-0338
http://www.mclean.harvard.edu

WebMD
http://www.webmd.com/

PARENTS' RESOURCES AND YOUTH MENTAL HEALTH ORGANIZATIONS

Active Minds on Campus
(202) 332-9595
http://www.activemindsoncampus.org/

American Academy for Child and Adolescent Psychiatry
(202) 966-7300
http://www.aacap.org/

Child and Adolescent Bipolar Foundation
http://www.bpkids.org/

Federation of Families for Children's Mental Health
http://www.ffcmh.org/

Juvenile Bipolar Research Foundation
(866) 333-JBRF (5273)
E-mail: info@jbrf.org
http://www.bpchildresearch.org/

SUICIDE PREVENTION

America Foundation for Suicide Prevention
(888) 333-AFSP (2377)
E-mail: inquiry@afsp.org
http://www.afsp.org/

National Suicide Prevention Lifeline
(800) 273-TALK (8255)
A twenty-four-hour, toll-free suicide prevention service available to anyone contemplating suicide or in suicidal crisis.

The Samaritans
Toll-free twenty-four-hour helpline: (877) 870-HOPE (4673)
http://www.samaritanshope.org/

ONLINE SUPPORT

Bipolar Significant Others
http://bpso.org/

Bipolar Support.org
http://bipolarsupport.org/

Bringchange2mind
http://bringchange2mind.org/

Harbor of Refuge
http://www.harbor-of-refuge.org/

Healthy Place
http://www.healthyplace.com/bipolar-disorder/menu-id-67/

Pendulum
www.pendulum.org

LEGAL ISSUES

The Bazelon Center for Mental Health Law
(202) 467-5730
E-mail: info@bazelon.org
http://www.bazelon.org/

BOOKS AND MAGAZINES

Magazine

BP Magazine
Subscription info: www.BPHope.com

The Basics

Cognitive-Behavioral Therapy for Bipolar Disorder, 2nd ed., by
   Monica Ramirez Basco (Guilford Press, 2007).
Desk Reference to the Diagnostic Criteria from DSM-IV-TR
   (American Psychiatric Association, 2000). Concise edition includes all the diagnostic criteria from *DSM-IV-TR*
   in an easy-to-use, spiral-bound format, and a pull-out chart
   of the *DSM-IV-TR* classification of psychiatric disorders.
*Manic-Depressive Illness: Bipolar Disorders and Recurrent Depres-
   sion*, by Frederick K. Goodwin and Kay Redfield Jamison
   (Oxford University Press, 2007). Highly technical and
   comprehensive.

General Information About Bipolar Disorder

Adult Bipolar Disorders: Understanding Your Diagnosis and Getting Help, by Mitzi Waltz (O'Reilly & Associates, 2002).

Bipolar Disorder: A Guide for Patients and Families, by Francis Mark Mondimore (Johns Hopkins University Press, 1999).

Bipolar Disorder for Dummies, by Candida Fink and Joe Kraynak (Wiley, 2004).

The Bipolar Disorder Survival Guide: What You and Your Family Need to Know, by David J. Miklowitz (Guilford Press, 2002).

The Bipolar Handbook, by Wes Burgess (Avery/Penguin, 2006).

Finding Your Bipolar Muse: How to Master Depressive Droughts and Manic Floods and Access Your Creative Power, by Lana R. Castle (Avalon, 2006).

The Friends and Family Bipolar Survival Guide, by Debra Meehl and Mark Meehl (Meehl Foundation Press, 2005).

Loving Someone with Bipolar Disorder, by Julie A. Fast and John Preston (New Harbinger, 2004).

An Unquiet Mind: A Memoir of Moods and Madness, by Kay Redfield Jamison (Vintage, 1997).

The Wiley Concise Guides to Mental Health: Bipolar Disorder, by Brian Quinn (Wiley, 2007).

Marriage, Relationships, and Communication

The Explosive Child, by Ross W. Greene (HarperCollins, 2005).

Tell Me No Lies, by Ellyn Bader and Peter Pearson (St. Martin's Press, 2001).

What Shamu Taught Me About Life, Love and Marriage, by Amy Sutherland (Random House, 2008).

Memoirs and Personal Accounts

A Brilliant Madness: Living with Manic Depressive Illness, by Patty Duke and Gloria Hochman (Bantam, 1997).

Electroboy: A Memoir of Mania, by Andy Behrman (Random House, 2003).

Madness: A Bipolar Life, by Marya Hornbacher (Mariner Books, 2009).

Manic: A Memoir, by Terri Cheney (Harper Paperbacks, 2009).

My Bipolar Road Trip in 4-D, by Lizzie Simon (Washington Square Press, 2003).

Scattershot: My Bipolar Family, by David Lovelace (Dutton Adult, 2008).

Sugar and Salt: My Life with Bipolar Disorder, by Jane Thompson (Authorhouse, 2006).

Ten Days in a Madhouse, by Nellie Bly (Norman L. Munro, 1887). In the late 1800s, a reporter infiltrated an infamous New York mental hospital to document conditions there firsthand. A fascinating look at an unenlightened approach to patient care. Available online at http://digital.library. upenn.edu/women/bly/madhouse/madhouse.html.

Win the Battle: The Three-Step Lifesaving Formula to Conquer Depression and Bipolar Disorder, by Bob Olsen and Melissa Olsen (Chandler House Press, 1999).

Negotiation

Beyond Reason: Using Emotions as You Negotiate, by Roger Fisher and Daniel Shapiro (Penguin Books, 2005).

Getting to Yes: Negotiating Agreement Without Giving In, by Bruce M. Patton, William L. Ury, and Roger Fisher (Houghton Mifflin Harcourt, 1992).

ABOUT THE AUTHORS

Chelsea Lowe is a professional writer and the author of *The Everything Health Guide to OCD*. She has written about mental health for *TV Guide*, the *Philadelphia Inquirer*, the *New York Daily News*, and the *Boston Globe*. Her personal essays and features have been heard on National Public Radio and seen in *Newsweek* and many other media.

Bruce M. Cohen, MD, PhD, is president and Psychiatrist in Chief Emeritus at McLean Hospital and the Robertson-Steele Professor of Psychiatry at Harvard Medical School. Currently, as director of the Frazier Research Institute at McLean, he leads a consortium of investigators and clinicians using laboratory, brain imaging, and clinical research techniques to develop new treatments of the most severe psychiatric disorders. His research activities focus particularly on the diagnosis and treatment of patients with psychotic and mood disorders, including bipolar disorders.

Following undergraduate studies at the Massachusetts Institute of Technology and graduate and medical studies at Case Western Reserve University, Dr. Cohen completed his residency training at McLean Hospital, where he established a clinical practice and an externally funded program of clinical and laboratory-based research. Cohen is the author of numerous publications on psychiatric diagnosis and treatment and on scientific findings relevant to psychiatry, including more than two hundred manuscripts of original research in peer-reviewed journals. He has won local and national awards for research, teaching, and clinical care. He has frequently been listed in local and national publications as one of the best doctors in America. He is a Fellow of the American College of Neuropsychopharmacolgy and a Distinguished Fellow of the American Psychiatric Association.

INDEX